VISIONARY
MIDDLE SCHOOLS

• • •

Signature Practices and the Power of Local Invention

VISIONARY
MIDDLE SCHOOLS

• • •

Signature Practices and the Power of Local Invention

CATHERINE COBB MOROCCO
Education Development Center, Inc.
Newton, Massachusetts

NANCY BRIGHAM
Rosenblum Brigham Associates
Philadelphia

CYNTHIA MATA AGUILAR
Education Development Center, Inc.
Newton, Massachusetts

Foreword by Michael Fullan

Teachers College, Columbia University
New York and London

Published by Teachers College Press, 1234 Amsterdam Avenue, New York, NY 10027

Library of Congress Cataloging-in-Publication Data

Morocco, Catherine Cobb.
    Visionary middle schools : signature practices and the power of local invention / Catherine Cobb Morocco, Nancy Brigham, Cynthia Mata Aguilar.
      p. cm.
    Includes bibliographical references and index.
    ISBN-13: 978-0-8077-4664-6 (alk paper)
    ISBN-10: 0-8077-4664-9 (alk. paper)
    ISBN-13: 978-0-8077-4663-9 (pbk. : alk. paper)
    ISBN-10: 0-8077-4663-0 (pbk. : alk. paper)
    1. Middle schools—United States—Case studies. 2. Middle school education.—United States—Case studies. 3. Educational change—United States—Case studies. I. Brigham, Nancy. II. Mata Aguilar, Cynthia. III. Title.
    LB1623.5.M67 2006
    373.236—dc22

                           2005054141

ISBN-13:	ISBN-10:
978-0-8077-4663-9 (paper)	0-8077-4663-0 (paper)
978-0-8077-4664-6 (cloth)	0-8077-4664-9 (cloth)

Printed on acid-free paper
Manufactured in the United States of America

13 12 11 10 09 08 07 06   8 7 6 5 4 3 2 1

Contents

Foreword

Morocco, Brigham, and Aguilar's concept of "Signature Practices" is brilliant. It is a concept with great sticky qualities. It captures an undeveloped theme in the literature, and calls forth an array of in-depth images of reform.

By starting with local innovation in the service of moral purpose, the authors end up identifying all the themes in today's reform field. The three case studies they present are rich in depth and coverage. In one way or the other, we see all the issues in the best of current innovative practices. In Dolphin Middle School, co-teaching and interdisciplinary work are the centerpiece; in Leonardo Da Vinci, they are Exhibitions and Technology; in Carter-Dean, investigations, inquiry, and interdisciplinary curriculum are the central focus. In all three cases, details particular to each context are revealed whereby the poor and the disabled are fully served, and everyone learns in a vibrant, active community. Inclusivity permeates the cultures of the three schools, each in its own way.

While each school is unique, the authors identify the common lessons. The work is deeply embedded across the school and its community; it is work that is customized to the needs of the individuals and subgroups that make up the school community. Above all, these schools are collaborative and engaging for all students and adults alike. Morocco and her colleagues have vividly captured what ownership looks like and how it is accomplished.

There is also a wonderfully clear and insightful depiction that "signature practice" is the centerpiece that draws on and incorporates local innovation, moral imperative, and schoolwide vision.

Morocco, Brigham, and Aguilar have written a book that has a double poignancy about it. On the one hand, there is the remarkable accomplishments in the three schools. On the other, there is the terrible mismatch between local innovation and Federal and State Policy. Time and again, the authors show how the two levels work at cross purposes. Despite this conflict, the book is optimistic about the staying power of carefully worked out local developments.

Visionary Middle Schools has so many powerful messages which are beautifully and forcefully presented.

—Michael Fullan

Preface

This book examines how three urban middle schools developed local solutions to a national crisis in the education of adolescents and the lessons those solutions offer current school and reform leaders. During the 1990s, poor achievement results and an alarming rise of troubling social behaviors—adolescent pregnancy and drug use—mobilized national panels, foundations, and school reform groups to spotlight young adolescents and invest in middle-grades reform. Through supreme efforts by school leaders, teachers, district leaders, and community groups, many schools reinvented themselves. Three of these schools are the subject of case studies presented here.

While these schools drew on research on learning and reform ideas in and beyond their districts, their solutions were essentially *local*, responsive to their particular student populations and cultures and to their particular district and state struggles and resources. Many hands helped shape the schools, yet the schools themselves were the *crucibles* in which solutions were fashioned to the challenges of educating young adolescents.

Counter to much wisdom of middle-grades reform in the 1990s, which viewed school reorganization as the starting point for change, these schools began with teaching and learning for all students. Each school is organized around a different schoolwide classroom practice that reflects and perpetuates that school's beliefs about learning. Each school embedded this instructional practice in a larger organizational or curricular structure that made it schoolwide.

Many case studies of successful schools tell of curriculum practices and leadership strengths that provide examples for reform. The different message from these school cases is that local designs—informed by thoughtful partnerships, research on learning, and the ideas of reformers beyond the schools—can result in solutions that are not best practices for all schools, but *signature practices* that help the schools to serve their particular students and communities.

In unearthing the schoolwide instructional practices of these high-performing schools, this book highlights a national dilemma. The local knowledge created by these middle schools and their reform partners is endangered by new reforms that threaten to narrow and homogenize the work of urban schools. Although the continuing high performance of these schools argues for the power of school and district decisions, current federal education policies are curtailing the time, resources, and will for local design. We have written the book to reveal qualities of local invention that have lessons for this millennium and raise questions about federalizing the process of school reform.

The successes and the challenges of these three vibrant, whole-school learning communities have much to offer other reforming middle schools. They also have lessons for American high schools, which have taken their place on the reform stage and will require supportive federal policies, research knowledge, and local invention to become excellent and equitable places of learning.

Acknowledgments

Our study of the three urban middle schools portrayed in this volume was supported by a grant to Education Development Center, Inc., from the U.S. Department of Education, Office of Special Education Programs (OSEP). The findings and our interpretations are our own and do not represent the views of the Department of Education. We are grateful for the support of OSEP program staff and of the other researchers in the Beacons of Excellence initiative.

Versions of these case studies have been published in journal articles for teachers and researchers and in a Web tour of one of the middle schools. In addition, we have presented these findings, together with photographs and video documentation, at national conferences on secondary school reform, schoolwide literacy, and access to a standards-based curriculum for students with disabilities.

Nancy Clark-Chiarelli contributed to the early conceptualization of the study and to gathering and analyzing survey and observation data from the schools. Her insights particularly inform our discussions of students with disabilities in these schools. Teri West helped us conduct a national search and application process to find these schools. We owe much to Nancy Ames for her reviews of earlier chapters and her contributions to our understanding of the middle-grades reform movement. David Riley has championed this work throughout and brought our results at various stages to his organization of district special education leaders across the country. Both David Riley and Leslie Hergert provided helpful comments on several chapters, and Cecilia Fernandes helped us prepare documents and communicate with the schools. We thank these EDC colleagues for their invaluable assistance.

Most of all, we want to acknowledge the principals, staff, teachers, students, parents, and district staff of the three schools and districts. They made us welcome; they shared their time, daily challenges, and creative problem solving with us. In a society that is still working toward social equity and equal access, they have created and sustained cultures of belonging and intellectual excitement for all of their students.

The Power of Local Innovation in Transforming Schools

> With No Child Left Behind, we don't have the luxury to explore at our own pace. 'Til I take my last breath, that's truly how I believe learning takes place. This pulling out of a piece, it doesn't stay. The teaching–learning process is a natural outgrowth of a big idea, and you explore the idea in an integrated fashion. But schools that fail to meet their [Adequate Yearly Progress—AYP] targets will be reconstituted. *They* will make our staff changes. *Thirty principals have been fired!*
> —Alvera Williams, principal, Carter-Dean Middle School

Alvera Williams is the founding principal of Carter-Dean Middle School. She is reliving a recent decision with her faculty to integrate periods of formal test preparation into the daily schedule three times a week. She says it is the most painful decision of her 30 years as a principal. For 10 years, her school has successfully brought inner-city, low-income Black students together with more-affluent suburban White students in a magnet school that partners with the city's science museums to educate students as "investigative learners." Williams's mission has been to design and sustain a learning community where students learn to explore difficult, important questions about their society.

Williams's middle school emerged from a first wave of middle-grades reform in the 1990s that stimulated local innovation in almost every state and district. Until 2004, Williams managed district pressure for rapid acceleration of students' test scores without giving away extensive instructional time to test preparation. Her philosophy was that deep subject-area work and students' knowledge would show up on the state tests without staff dedicating extensive time to test preparation, other than to teach students multiple choice and essay formats. But in 2004, because of pressures on the district from the state's implementation of No Child Left Behind

(NCLB), the school needed to increase its language arts scores by 19% and its mathematics scores by 10%. Williams is indignant that NCLB leads to "punishing schools if they do not make their targets."

NCLB represents a second wave of reform, likened by some to a tidal wave, that is reshaping schools across the country. While successful schools of the 1990s share with NCLB a commitment to equal educational opportunity, NCLB imposes federal solutions to the challenges of reforming schools. NCLB was presented as a strategy for equity intended to reach every group of traditionally marginalized students, including students with disabilities. It is, however, a system of high-stakes testing that institutes federal controls over the setting of standards for success and failure. NCLB requires the federal government to withhold funds if states, districts, and schools do not comply with those standards. Penalties for noncompliance are prescribed by law.

Williams's indignation reflects the pain of having to choose between following her most deeply held philosophical and *moral* commitment to her students and responding to a threat of being "reconstituted"—taken over by the district—which is the most extreme penalty under NCLB. She chose to respond to intensified achievement demands by balancing her commitments to student inquiry and to state standards for accountability. Other school leaders have responded differently. An assistant principal of another innovative middle school, who was required by her district to shift to pull-out programs for students with low performance on statewide tests, abandoned her original vision of effective schooling. "Everything we've been doing is wrong," she decided, despite the school's 10 years of academic success with a low-income student population.

Critics of NCLB who share Williams's concern are calling for national attention to documented, unintended consequences of NCLB mandates for the very student populations the law is intended to benefit. The NCLB mandate that every state use a single test in reading and mathematics for school accountability is undoing the thoughtful and varied assessment systems that districts and states developed during the 1990s. Another concern is that students with disabilities and other low-performing students are being "disappeared" from the early high school grades by being counseled out or otherwise encouraged to drop out (Darling-Hammond, 2004).

The most profound unintended consequence, critics argue, is that NCLB "usurps the right of local communities to define the attributes of a sound education" (Meier, 2004, p. 71). In a historic break from a tradition of local educational autonomy, NCLB assumes that children, families, educational professionals, and their communities cannot be trusted to make critical decisions about their own schools (Meier, 2004).

This book examines three urban middle schools that emerged from the first wave of reform in the 1990s with a strong vision that translated into a coherent and highly innovative approach to educating young adolescents. Each school fashioned a different approach to realizing a common underlying vision of a good middle school. The three schools serve as examples of the power of local invention, informed by a strong vision of student learning and research-based practice, and fueled by a moral imperative.

One school is Dolphin Middle School, in an economically diverse community in the south. It is also the most culturally diverse of the three, with a mix of White, Latino, and African American students, including a large group of Latino children of migrant workers. A second is Leonardo Da Vinci Middle School, situated in one of the most densely populated urban districts in the northeast. Ninety-five percent of its students are Latino, from a wide variety of Caribbean and Central and South American countries. The third is Williams's school, Carter-Dean Investigative Learning Center Middle School, a magnet school in the midwest. Sixty percent of Carter-Dean students are African American from low-income, inner-city families, and 40% are White students from relatively affluent suburbs.

All three of these schools drew on research on learning, national reform ideas, and strategies to devise schools and schoolwide instructional practices—in this book we call them *signature practices*—that work for their particular communities, social challenges, and student populations.

THE REFORM CONTEXT FOR LOCAL INNOVATION

The innovative practices at these three schools emerged as the schools and their districts were each grappling with their own local reform challenges at a time of national ferment and conversation about young adolescents and middle-grades schools. National concerns about how young adolescents were being educated led to the forging of an integrated set of goals for middle schools. At the same time, a national movement to include students with disabilities in the least restrictive learning environments was bringing students with disabilities into middle schools and increasing the academic diversity of classrooms. These movements, together with the emergence of high-stakes testing, placed middle schools under extreme pressure to change—the question was how and the answer was local invention.

The 1980s brought a growing awareness that early adolescence is not just a turbulent transition on the way to maturity, but is itself a critical period of growth and development. Complex, abstract thinking becomes possible at this age. At the same time, youths are searching for ways to define themselves, and desires for social acceptance and adventure make them vulnerable to risky behavior (Irvin, 1995). Reports about low school performance and high rates of pregnancy, dropping out, substance abuse, and school violence drew national attention to this age group and catalyzed a series of reforms. National assessments of eighth graders in the late 1980s found that only 11% were able to understand relatively complicated written information, including information related to topics they studied at school. Only 13% of eighth graders wrote adequate or better essays, that is, essays that included sufficient information to achieve the required objective (Campbell, Voelkl, & Donahue, 1997).

Several books and reports of that era argued that schools must respond to young adolescents' special developmental strengths and needs. Lipsitz (1984) used four case studies to launch a national dialogue on schools for young adolescents, arguing in favor of "threshold" criteria for excellent middle schools. The Carnegie Council on Adolescent Development produced an influential report called *Turning Points* (1989), which reflected this urgency and argued that schools for young adolescents—too often miniature high schools—needed to respond to this turbulent and important time of growth with total change. The smaller learning environments, advisories, and mentoring programs proposed in the report would ensure that every student was known well by at least one adult. Caring adults would be available to talk about social and emotional issues that threaten a student's well-being and academic productivity. Working in teams, teachers could connect curricula across the subjects. Flexible scheduling and grouping would enable students to work cooperatively and intensively on important projects and topics.

Reflecting many ideas from that research (MacIver, 1990; MacIver & Epstein, 1993), the National Middle School Association (1995) presented its image of "developmentally responsive" middle-level schools. The middle school model that emerged from these calls for action in the early 1990s emphasized a set of organizational structures that would create a nurturing learning environment for young adolescents.

Fragmented Middle-Grades Reforms

The middle-grades model—highlighting developmentally responsive ways to organize schools—did not, as it turned out, lead to improved academic learning. Having advisories, teaming, and block scheduling did not necessarily lead teachers to lecture less to their students or design intellectually stimulating curriculum units. Critics argued that the middle-grades structures were a "checklist approach" to school change that did not focus on teaching and learning. They said that schools were being asked to restructure around students' vulnerabilities without also emphasizing their intellectual generativity. Williamson and Johnston (1999) challenged what they called the "middle grades orthodoxy"—an unquestioning allegiance to middle school components such as teaming, advisories and interdisciplinary curricula, rather than making those approaches serve academic goals. "Reforming middle grades programs must be driven by student achievement. . . . Teams are not implemented just to have teams. Grouping is not modified just to change practice. Such changes take place because they contribute to greater student achievement and success" (p. 15).

Another stream of reform was the standards movement, which brought new waves of standards-based curricula and assessments. Catalyzed by the National Council of Teachers of Mathematics (1989), professional mathematics communities gathered to define the habits of mind and methods of mathematics instruction that would build students' mathematical thinking. Science educators (National Science Foundation, 1997) and language specialists (National Council of Teachers of English and International Reading Association, 1996) formed local groups of teachers and content-area reform leaders around the country to generate lists of important outcomes and develop standards. Curriculum designs followed that demonstrated for teachers how standards should look in practice.

With changes in curriculum and teaching approaches came new ways of thinking about assessing learning. Assessment standards often were paired with content standards in order to ensure that assessments were aligned with curriculum goals of deep understanding. A combination of assessment approaches emerged from local needs. Reformers sought to make assessments fit the new curricula and ways of teaching and to allow students many ways of representing what they knew. Other groups were focusing more on equity concerns, particularly groups working on urban school reforms. Emerging programs, such as the Yale School Development Program, sought to engage schools in the full development of inner-city children most at risk for school failure, in partnership with parents and community child development organizations (Comer, Haynes, Joyner, & Ben-Avie, 1996).

These three streams of reforms—school structures, standards-based curriculum and assessment, and equity—redefined the critical elements of middle-grades education. Yet these streams typically were not connected at the school level. Foundation funding for middle-grades reform reflected this divergence of ideas and focus. The Lily Endowment, Inc., promoted changes in district thinking and visions of young adolescent development. The Carnegie Foundation gave grants to states and schools to implement *Turning Points* recommendations and also raised concerns about social equity. The Edna McConnell Clark Foundation pushed for intellectual challenge in schools, and the W. K. Kellogg Foundation initiatives focused on district planning for change and statewide coalitions for middle-grades reform. Sharing middle-grades education as a priority, these foundations pursued different avenues of reform.

An Integrated Vision for Middle Schools

Representatives of the four foundations mentioned above and of organizations engaged in middle-grades reform came together in May 1994 to talk about their work. Realizing that no shared vision underlay their disparate initiatives, they made a decision virtually unprecedented for foundations: to hold a series of meetings and form a shared vision. Their goal was to "speak with one voice" (Lipsitz, Mizell, Jackson, & Austin, 1997). Calling themselves "the shepherds of school reform," the organizational representatives met four times between May 3, 1994 and December 14, 1995.

At the first of the four conversations, as they called their meetings, participants realized that they shared a sense of urgency for change (Education Development Center [EDC], 1994). One participant stated the issue:

> For change to occur, you need a genuine belief that bad stuff is happening for kids right now. You need a feeling of distress. You also need a climate of trust in which you can say it's not all OK. You need permission to tell the truth and a willingness to talk about and change what you do. You need to move from defensiveness to openness. (Ch. 1, p. 23)

By the time of this meeting, the first wave of middle school reform—the "bubbly brew" of ideas, as they called it, was already fermenting, fueled in large part by *Turning Points*. As a result, this meeting and subsequent ones were at times arduous discussions about what the big reform ideas were and how they fit together.

Two big ideals for excellent middle schools were prominent in early meetings, a developmentally responsive school climate and an intellectually rigorous curriculum. The tension occurred around prioritizing and sequencing these ideals. One person argued that a developmentally responsive climate and school structures were the foundation and starting point for reform, and that everything else would follow: "The idea of talking about raising student achievement before the structures are in place is like talking to homeless people about interior decorating" (EDC, 1994, Ch. 2, p. 11). Others responded that classroom instruction had to be a primary focus, if not *the* primary focus, from the very beginning. The fear was that structures and components would become the objective rather than student learning. "How do you press the issue of middle schools producing good people and good citizens without letting them off the hook of producing people who have the intellectual wherewithal to take care of themselves and their families?" (Ch. 2, p. 15).

As participants argued about the primacy of developmental responsiveness or academic excellence, another expert called the group's attention to a third big idea—social equity. Participants linked this idea to the concept of democratic schools, where all students, including those most marginalized by poverty, color, and/or language status, have equal opportunity for a voice and for academic success. One of the conversation participants argued, "Caring is not enough; academics are not enough; mechanics are not enough. Success for every kid is the goal" (EDC, 1994, Ch. 4, pp. 5–6).

By the end of the second conversation, the group concluded that a commitment to social justice was among the nonnegotiables of their middle school framework. Social equity linked to academic opportunity needed to be the driving moral force of the vision.

From intense and sometimes contentious conversations emerged a three-part vision of middle schools that would integrate developmental responsiveness, academic excellence, and social equity. Calling these the "tripod" of middle-grades reform, the group published what they called a "manifesto," intended to shape policy, funding, and district and school change across the country (see Figure 1.1). While the group presented their manifesto as three ideas of equal importance, the question of what comes first and how all three become integral to a school's vision and practice was still unanswered.

The foundation representatives anticipated other questions: What forces outside the schools may work against these big goals? Will national standards advance or impede the progress of middle schools toward this integrated set of goals? Will standards advance the cause of social equity and social justice? Some foundation participants expressed misgivings about standards. Even when we have standards, how will they be used? One group can use them to sort people. Another can use them to ensure that all students reach the benchmarks.

Another question was how to get from an integrated vision to actual school change. The foundation representatives discussed ways to translate these goals into practice and whether reform leaders should advocate for specific models and approaches. They proposed a new national reform organization, to be called the National Middle-Grades Forum, as a strategy for making the manifesto public and guiding middle schools toward integrated models of change.

Figure 1.1. A Manifesto: Goals for Middle-Grades Reform

Developmental responsiveness: They (schools) act on the knowledge that the imperatives of early adolescent development are too compelling to be denied. They adapt school practices to this knowledge.

Academic excellence: Rather than becoming enmeshed in changing climate and structures, high-performing schools know that these critical components of the reform process enable deeper instructional changes to occur. The schools employ those environmental changes as mechanisms for realizing the ultimate goal of middle-grades reform: enabling young adolescents to achieve at high levels academically while developing well socially, physically, and emotionally.

Social equity: A belief that disadvantaged students can perform at high levels and a commitment to making that happen are fundamental to the pursuit of school improvement. We have seen schools break the powerful grip that poverty and race exert on academic performance. If some schools can accomplish this success, others can as well.

Source: Adapted from "Speaking with One Voice" by Lipsitz, Mizell, Jackson, & Austin, 1997.

Students with Disabilities in the Reform

Students with disabilities were not a focus of the conversations between the representatives of foundations and middle-grades organizations. Nevertheless, they were the heart and center of a concurrent movement to include more students with disabilities in the general education curriculum and classroom. Classrooms of the 1990s already were including the majority of young adolescents with identified mild learning disabilities (LD), although many parents of those students had concerns about the adequacy of the academic support their children were receiving.

Parents of students with cognitive and more significant disabilities, who were being educated primarily in separate classrooms, began advocating for their children to be included in general education classrooms as well. They argued that their children needed to be in the least restrictive setting, not only to have normal social development, but also to have access to an academically relevant curriculum. Having a disability, they said, magnifies the young adolescent's risk of academic failure and therefore limits his or her educational and life opportunities.

The 1997 reauthorization of the Individuals with Disabilities Education Act (IDEA) reiterated a national commitment to educate students with disabilities in classrooms with their more typically achieving peers. Schools became accountable for including students with disabilities in the intellectual work of the classroom, providing them academic support to succeed, and reporting their academic results on high-stakes tests. This movement defined inclusion as a critical aspect of social equity in schooling.

By the middle to late 1990s, a strong research base was emerging that identified instructional approaches that particularly benefit students with learning disabilities. The peer support inherent in cooperative learning helps students with LD by clarifying assignments, modeling performance, explaining ideas, providing feedback and correction, and scaffolding problem-solving efforts (Englert et al., 1995; Fuchs et al., 1997; Morocco, Hindin, & Aguilar, 2002; Palincsar & Klenk, 1992). Middle school students with LD are able to write better-structured and more elaborate essays when they work in cooperative pairs (Wong, Butler, Ficzere, & Kuperis, 1996), and they benefit from instruction in reading comprehension (Williams, 1998). The challenge for teachers and schools was how to integrate these effective strategies into the changing middle school curriculum and instruction.

At about this time, Education Development Center (EDC), Inc., launched an organization to support urban school district leaders as they struggled to transform special education. Now a national network of more than 100 urban school districts, the Urban Special Education Leadership Collaborative began with a group of 11 urban districts. Those pioneer districts joined together around this mission statement:

> The Collaborative is a network of special and general education leaders working together to improve outcomes for students with disabilities in the nation's urban schools. It was founded in 1994 on the premise that mutual support, sharing of information and resources, and planning/problem-solving partnerships will strengthen each member district's ability to improve educational results and life opportunities for children and youth with disabilities in urban schools.

The conversation participants did not explicitly discuss including students with disabilities as part of their vision of a middle school, and, as a reflection of the times, the Collaborative fastened on only one part of the tripod—social equity. That is, they wanted schools to feel an imperative to include students with disabilities in the academic and social life of the school. It was left to the middle schools themselves to define policies and identify practices that would integrate the goals of middle-grades reform and the sprit of IDEA.

VISIONARY MIDDLE SCHOOLS

"Show us schools that work!" became a call from the networks of middle-grades reformers and schools in the National Middle-Grades Forum and in the growing Collaborative, both housed within Education Development Center, Inc. In 1997, the Forum called for reform leaders and school leaders to nominate "Schools to Watch"—middle schools on a trajectory of change that reflected the middle-grades developmental structures and movement toward academic improvement for all groups of students. Out of an extensive search, the Forum identified schools and posted descriptions on the Forum website.

Also in 1997, the U.S. Department of Education, Office of Special Education Programs (OSEP) launched a research initiative, Beacons of Excellence, asking researchers to identify and study schools that could provide positive models of access and academic success for students with disabilities. The idea was that lessons from successful schools at all levels would inform the knowledge-base for continuing reform. The Collaborative urged researchers to focus on positive *urban* examples, seeing urban centers as the most critical opportunities for reform because of the concentration of students with disabilities in their schools. Providing the highest quality middle-grades education for all students was, they argued, particularly challenging for schools that lacked the resources and preconditions for reform. Seeing in-depth examples of good schools for students with disabilities would be of great help for urban school leaders.

EDC's Beacons of Excellence Project

EDC's Beacons of Excellence Project was granted the funds to find and study visionary middle schools from 1997 through 2000. The project brought together the goals and vision of the middle-grades reform movement and the desire of special education leaders for examples of successful, inclusive schools. Of the six proposals that OSEP funded, only EDC's focused on the middle grades. The project launched a yearlong search for Beacons middle schools, using as a framework the tripod of developmental responsiveness, academic excellence, and social equity. The project would identify schools that were located in urban communities and, as a part of their goals for social equity, educated students with disabilities within diverse and heterogeneous general education classrooms.

Using a "mixed methods" research approach (Johnson & Onwuegbuzie, 2004), described in Appendix A, project staff conducted a national search for a year. From 40 applicants and eight semifinalist sites, we selected three urban middle schools in three different parts of the country. As the opening brief descriptions of the schools suggest, each school serves a different kind of urban population, one culturally diverse, one primarily Latino, and one a balance of White and African American students. While the three schools were founded in the 1990s, each has a different reform story catalyzed by a different social or educational crisis.

Signature practice as the central finding. We searched for schools that appeared, from their applications and our site visits, to embrace at a broad level the three big ideas of the middle-grades reform vision: developmental responsiveness, academic excellence, and social equity. And we confirmed the presence of this vision in our extended study of the schools. We can theorize that we found them not only because we were looking for this vision, but also because the "bubbly brew" of middle-grades reform ideas entered the collective consciousness of astute school leaders and married with their own vision of reform.

The striking finding of our study is that the three schools all translated this general shared vision into a single schoolwide approach that is coherent and consistent across the school. Each school has what we call a *signature practice* that organizes learning for all students. To make the vision fit their particular population, these leaders invented a schoolwide practice, a way of teaching and learning that pervades every subject area, grade level, and classroom. Furthermore, the schools created completely *different* signature practices. In Williams's school the signature practice consists of investigations of big social and scientific questions; in Dolphin Middle School the signature practice is co-teaching by special education and general education teachers; in Leonardo Da Vinci the signature practice is technology-supported exhibitions of student learning.

While these practices are not novel inventions in the middle school world—they do exist in various forms in other schools and districts—the particular features of these innovations are unique to these schools. Most important, each school's signature practice is responsive to the particular needs of the student population and to its own district crises or reform needs. The practice in each school responds to the developmental needs of the particular groups of young adolescents in that community. It provides a route to academic excellence and creates a socially equitable learning community for all of the groups of students that make up that community. While the signature practice at the core of instruction in each school reflects research on learning and is present in other reform communities, the particular shape, features, and meaning of the practice are essentially *local* and reflective of the culture of that school.

The signature practice is of interest in itself as an inclusive practice. It is also the window through which we can see the deeper culture of the school and how the school is able to achieve academic excellence with all of its groups of students. Our use of the term *culture* builds from Geertz's

(1973) definition of culture as a "historically transmitted pattern of meanings embodied in symbols, a system of inherited conceptions expressed in symbolic forms by means of which men communicate, perpetuate, and develop their knowledge about and attitudes toward life" (p. 89). We have widened his definition to refer to meanings that define the purpose and ways of learning and interacting that are pervasive in a school. These schools have "cultures of excellence, belonging, and justice" because they provide students who tend to be marginalized in our society by poverty, minority status, language proficiency, and/or disability a place in an academically rigorous learning community.

To understand why the practice has rooted in the school and what it means to participants is to understand why the school has succeeded against the odds associated with urban poverty and the challenges inherent in educating increasingly diverse learners. The practice grew out of an imperative for change.

What fueled the local invention of signature practices? The leadership of the three Beacons schools was driven by a vision so pervasive and intense that it amounted to a kind of moral imperative. In the ethics of Immanuel Kant, a moral imperative stems from the belief that human will commands respect for humanity as an end in itself; that belief in turn motivates action for the common good. Such good will, according to Kant's argument, is the only thing in the world that we can call *good* without qualification (Johnson, 1996).

In defining moral imperative at the school level, Fullan (2003) argues that the only worthwhile purpose for school reform is a *moral* one—transforming schools so that they are equitable systems: "Moral purpose of the highest order is having a system where all students learn, the gap between high and low performance becomes greatly reduced, and what people learn enables them to be successful citizens and workers in a morally based knowledge society" (p. 29). Our research team found in the three Beacons schools a set of leaders who reflected that purpose and who shared that moral imperative with all of the founders of the schools and with each school's continuing staff and families.

The principals' beliefs, stemming from their own backgrounds and philosophy, led them to insist on a school curriculum, culture, and climate that nurtured each student's ability to learn. They expressed their beliefs with a force of moral purpose, righteous indignation, and a keen sense of the injustices of society. This in turn nurtured a drive to create a shared approach to teaching and learning in the school that served as a vehicle and embodiment of the school's moral purpose. The resulting signature practice contributes to high performance because of the meaning and value it has for participants. The signature practice reveals students' competence and levels the playing field to provide students with disabilities and other vulnerable students access to the curriculum.

The signature practice is the centerpiece of these schools, yet it does not operate in isolation. The leaders embedded the practice in larger structures and practices that support it and make it work for all groups of students, including students with disabilities. In contrast to the reform view that organizational structures are the necessary foundation of the middle school, these schools placed their instructional approach at the center and designed supportive organizational structures around it (see Figure 1.2). Co-teaching is embedded in the major structure of interdisciplinary teaming in Dolphin; exhibitions are supported by advanced uses of technology in Leonardo Da Vinci; and investigations take place within interdisciplinary curriculum units at Carter-Dean. These structures and additional features help to make rigorous academic learning accessible to all students.

ORGANIZATION OF THE CHAPTERS

The three following chapters, 2 through 4, present case studies that tell the story of each school through the lens of its signature practice. Each case chapter opens with a description of the practice at work in the classroom. One or more students with disabilities are present in each vignette. The case then describes the beliefs behind the practice, the emergence of the practice in the founding of the school, and early choices of the school leaders. The case histories portray how the school and district leadership took advantage of ruptures in "business as usual" caused by desegregation

Figure 1.2. Signature Practices and Support Structures

School	Signature practice	Major supporting structure
Dolphin Middle School	Co-teaching	Interdisciplinary teams
Leonardo Da Vinci Middle School	Exhibitions	Technology tools
Carter-Dean Middle School	Investigations	Interdisciplinary curricula

mandates, statewide assessments, and demographic changes. In all three schools, school leaders and staff deliberately crystallized a philosophy of learning during a period of struggle, and thought through how to plant that philosophy in their school.

We unpack the signature practice to reveal what it demands of students and the features that make intellectual work accessible to students with limited English literacy, students with disabilities, and, in two of the schools, students who recently have immigrated to this country. The cases identify continuing challenges that teachers and school leaders face—managing changes in leadership, surviving "White flight" to charter schools and the suburbs, mediating student–student conflict, reaching parents, and responding to higher standards and statewide assessments.

Following the case studies, Chapter 5 draws on our examination of the three school cases to describe commonalities across the schools. We describe the major characteristics of signature practices in these schools and provide a theory of the reform forces that together generate a signature practice. Finally, we discuss the relevance of these schools of the 1990s to the current reform crises and climate of reform after 5 years in the new millennium. We return to Alvera Williams's dilemma of how to manage external pressures for high achievement while developing the best education for a particular local population of students. We ask what can and should be the roles of federal and state policy in promoting transformation through local innovation.

Appendix A describes the research methodology used to study the schools. We describe the sometimes rocky journey that we underwent to identify three school partners, unearth what was happening in each school, explain the school's resilience and the coherence of the many parts of the school, and understand the school's compelling commitment to its students and the academic success it achieved. Without providing an overly technical methodology discussion, we share the process and some of the challenges of getting to know a school.

Appendix B presents the survey instrument described in Appendix A, which we used to ask students, teachers, and parents for their viewpoint on students sense of safety and belonging in the school, availability of appropriate academic help for individual students, the academic rigor of the school, parents' own sense of importance and belonging, and students' motivation to learn. Developed by Abt Associates to evaluate schools in Detroit, Chicago, and Cleveland that were using James Comer's Yale School Development Program, the survey asks the same or similar questions of students, teachers, and families to assess the extent of agreement among these different members of the school community.

Co-Teaching in Dolphin Middle School

"Okay, today you're going to make up riddles to stump the class."

Two teachers stand in front of a seventh-grade class in Dolphin Middle School to set up an activity in which students will write geography riddles in small groups. Over the past month, students have been studying Africa by drawing relief/elevation maps, selecting a country or group to study in more depth, reading about the country from Internet and print sources, and designing giant postage stamps of their African countries to represent some feature of the culture of the country. Their final reports on their selected countries—bright travel brochures that integrate text and computer graphics—cover a side wall. An eye-catching brochure on Egypt poses the question, "What's inside a pyramid?" A *National Geographic* world map covers a 4' × 6' space on the back wall. Books on various African countries are grouped on long bookshelves to create a classroom library. Several computers make the Internet continually available for research.

"Countdown! 15, 14, 13, 12, 11, 10. Okay, ladies and gentlemen, thank you. I appreciate how every desk is cleared off." When every eye is on the two teachers standing at the front of the class, Sam Marcus, the geography teacher, presents the day's challenge: "Here is your goal. You are trying to design a riddle for the class. You will come up with a set of clues to physical features of a particular geographical area or an important landmark or to the characteristics of a political leader. You need to write down eight clues, going from the hardest clue to the easiest." Hannah Headley, the special education teacher, chimes in to get feedback on what students understand: "What would be an example of a landmark?" Students answer, "The Sphinx, the Aswan Dam, mosques."

The two teachers are using the riddling activity to strengthen students' recall of what they have learned and to connect important information about the African leaders, topographies, and cultures they have been studying. Although this content is part of the district's seventh-grade social studies curriculum and closely tied to Florida standards, composing riddles is the two teachers' invention. The competition and the small-group interaction fuel students' information sharing. The riddle format, with clues of descending difficulty, pushes students to think strategically about what information is likely to be most and least familiar to their classmates.

The teachers work together seamlessly to make the riddling task clear to every student. Headley draws out further ideas to set up the activity: "What are some countries we have studied?" Students call out, "Egypt, the Sudan . . ." Headley praises them, "They know their geography!" and then adds, "Oh my goodness, look at all of these hands. . . . There are many other countries. If you're not sure, just *ask*." She draws a large graphic on the whiteboard to show the categories students can use (leaders, landmarks, peoples, geographical areas) and sample details in each category. When a student says "Kadafi" as an example of a leader, she says that she will spell it phonetically. When one student suggests "Masai" as an example under "peoples," another boy announces that "the Masai drink cow's blood!" and looks around for attention. Headley turns the provocation into a question about local cultures: "An intriguing detail about Masai culture. Think about what else we learned about the Masai that might explain why this is a good solution to a problem."

Marcus draws a second graphic organizer on the board to illustrate how to write clues that range from easiest to hardest. While he explains this continuum, Headley surveys the room to see who may be confused. She moves to the board to get students to generate possible sources of information. She writes, "Where can I find information?" and underneath writes "ATLAS, textbook, Mr. M., the Internet," as students call out possibilities. Satisfied that students understand enough to begin, the teachers move on to grouping: "Now choose your partners."

Terry, a burly student with learning disabilities who often needs additional help, quickly finds a group. Marbella, who recently was mainstreamed into the class from the English as a second language (ESOL) program, works with Aracelli, who is fluently bilingual, and Letty, who joined the class late in the year because her parents are agricultural workers who migrate from one part of the country to another. Stan hovers by his desk, looking around, but does not move to get a partner. He has mild autism. While he brings great enthusiasm to the class and retains an unusual amount of information, he sometimes needs help working with other students. He also has difficulty with changes of routine and tends to participate impulsively, feeling that the other students are "not so smart." Headley watches him until he finally walks over to a boy sitting by himself, and they work together. As Marcus and Headley move around assisting students, Terry asks if they can use their books. The teachers confer audibly about this—as though publicly validating their partnership—and decide together that students can consult books and notes while they develop and guess the riddles.

The resulting riddle topics range from Victoria Falls to King Tut to the Sahel. When students have completed their clues and are ready to stump the class, two students pose their questions: (1) I'm over 69,481 square miles, (2) I am a physical feature, (3) I border Uganda, (4) I am not man-made, (5) I am part of the Nile." Their classmates take turns guessing until, finally, one gets it correct. Next, it is Terry and his partner's turn. They give their clues: "(1) I have a beard." A student guesses incorrectly. "(2) I wear a mask." A student shouts out, "Tut! I got it on the second clue!"

Marcus and Headley regularly cooperate to teach—that is, co-teach—a class that includes new migrant students barely familiar with how Dolphin classrooms work, children of recent immigrants who still struggle with English, and students with varied abilities and disabilities. Their approach is not unique in the school. Dolphin's administrators, teachers, and district personnel chose co-teaching as the model of instruction at the school's inception in order to support a diverse student population without dividing students into honors and regular classrooms or creating separate classrooms for students with disabilities. The only students who work separately for a time are those who come with no English—and they soon move into regular classrooms. Teachers find that co-teaching is a way to support a wide range of students in a heterogeneous class.

Although co-teaching does not look exactly the same across Dolphin classrooms, it usually involves an equal partnership between the general education teacher and the special education teacher. Teachers co-teach in every content area in order to give students with these diverse backgrounds as many entries as possible into complex content. Classroom co-teaching is the heart of the school. Teachers team in an intricate partnership aimed at engaging every student in connecting information, understanding concepts, and thinking about what they know. Because co-teaching is embedded in interdisciplinary teaming, it reaches beyond the classroom to team planning sessions, budget managing, and connections to parents. It also connects to systems of crisis management and family support that extend help for students into the home and community.

Several features, displayed in Figure 2.1, provide a schoolwide context for co-teaching and connect it with the supports for teachers and students that make it a strong practice for a diverse student body. Co-teaching is cooperative classroom teaching with several features that give it coherence and anchor it within Dolphin's organization and philosophy. The key features of co-teaching at Dolphin include

Figure 2.1. Co-Teaching at Dolphin

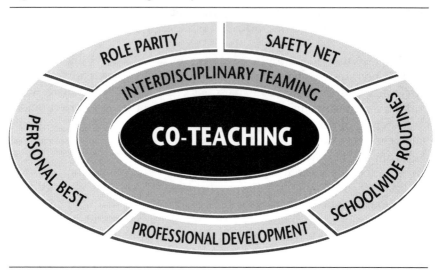

- *Interdisciplinary teams.* Teams include a special education teacher who co-teaches with each of the other teachers.
- *Parity and flexibility in co-teaching.* Two qualified teachers—a special education teacher and a content teacher—plan and teach together.
- *Joint professional development.* All teachers participate in common learning experiences to build teaching skills.
- *Schoolwide orientation routine.* Teachers have specific ways of organizing the flow of the class to make activities and expectations explicit.
- *A "personal best" curriculum.* Teachers connect personally with all students and explicitly teach a character curriculum.
- *A safety net of services.* Teams provide a wide range of services for students and families that help students to be ready for learning.

In recent years, co-teaching has been under critical scrutiny by some educators because of its expensive staffing costs and limited evidence of its impact on student learning and outcomes (Cook & Friend, 1995; Rice & Zigmond, 2000; Zigmond, 2001; Zigmond & Magiera, 2001). A meta-analysis of six co-teaching studies, however, found that co-teaching is a moderately effective procedure for influencing student outcomes and that it has the greatest impact on achievement in the areas of reading and language arts (Murawski & Swanson, 2001). Moreover, the conditions in which co-teaching has been studied may not reflect the best models or its real potential as an inclusive and integrative practice.

In most of the co-teaching pairs that researchers have studied, the special education teacher has not taken a substantive instructional role and often interacts with students as an aide would (Dieker, 2001). The general practice is for a few innovative teachers to implement co-teaching piecemeal, rather than as a schoolwide practice focused on complex learning related to state standards (Murawski & Swanson, 2001; Walther-Thomas, 1997). Dolphin is an exception in extending co-teaching across the school and embedding it consistently within interdisciplinary teaming and a standards-based curriculum.

The way Dolphin contextualizes co-teaching within interdisciplinary teaming is probably the most important feature of its signature practice. It is this that enables general and special education teachers to reach their very diverse groups of learners. In the words of Tina, a special education teacher, "What happens [with students] on those teams each and every day is indescribable. It happens in a look, in a brief conversation, in the hallway, at the side of a student's desk, asking him if everything is okay. That is truly the heart of Dolphin Middle School. Everything goes on in those teams, including inclusion and co-teaching. You see, co-teaching is *teaming within the classroom.*"

MEET AN INCLUSIVE MIDDLE SCHOOL

School buses stream from the interstate onto a side road that runs across a broad area of wetlands and brush to a sprawling one-story school, Dolphin Middle School. Home to 550 students in grades 6, 7, and 8, the school lies on acres of open country in one of the largest counties on the Gulf Coast. Miner County, 2,025 square miles, is a mixed-income county with retirement communities, migrant families, and more-affluent families. The school is 8 miles from Manlo Island, one of the highest income communities in the area, where the affluent retire and American and European tourists flock to beaches, golf resorts, and shopping malls.

Dolphin and one other middle school serve the poorest students in Miner County. Dolphin used to be more diverse. It was distinctive in the mid-1990s as a mixed-income, culturally diverse school until, in 1998, Manlo Island parents withdrew their children—150 students, all White—to form their own charter school. This change is reminiscent of the "White flight" from the northern cities in the 1960s, when White families flocked to the suburbs to avoid proximity to poverty and urban lifestyles. The large majority of Dolphin students now come from low-income minority families whose homes cluster in nearby neighborhoods and along a highway that crosscuts the county. Dolphin parents are service workers in tourist businesses, landscapers who manicure the lush South Coast landscapes, and migrant families who work for the local farming industry.

Because of its proximity to the South Coast, Miner County is a gateway into the United States for migrant workers and their families. They come from many Central American countries as well as from Mexico, Haiti, and the Dominican Republic to seek jobs in the fields picking oranges, grapefruit, and tomatoes. Their pay cannot begin to compare with American minimum wage standards. Tomato pickers are willing to work under the scorching southern sun to earn 40 cents for every 32-pound bucket. To earn $50 in a day, a local picker must harvest 2 tons, or 125 buckets, of tomatoes. The relationship between the workers and the farmers has not always been smooth, and there is a long history of legal battles between the farmers and migrant councils for the civil rights of migrant workers, including the right to adequate working conditions and housing (DeWind, 1998).

Dolphin Students

Following the withdrawal of the Manlo students, Dolphin became 54% Hispanic, 34% Black, and 12% White. Immigrant households include Hispanic families from Mexico and Central and South America as well as the Dominican Republic and Puerto Rico, and Black families from Haiti and Jamaica. Poverty is a common thread and, as a result, Dolphin is a Title I school, with 83% of students receiving free and/or reduced-price lunch. English is a second language for 27% of the students. Some are ESOL students with little or no knowledge of English. Others, like Marbella, originally from Mexico, have been in the United States for several years and have learned how to read and write in English but still use Spanish at home.

Migrant students make up 23% of Dolphin's student population. These students' families are of two kinds: those who travel extensively following the agricultural harvest cycle in different regions of the United States, and those who stay to work the Florida fields. The travel season for those who work across the country begins with harvests up north and in states such as Illinois and Michigan, where they pick strawberries and cherries. Throughout the summer months and into early fall, they follow the migrant circuit, finally returning to their homes in late October and early November. Their summer homes range from cinderblock one-room houses to apartments to trailers.[1] For those who remain in Miner County, work lies in the vast orange groves and tomato fields. Days typically begin at 4:00 in the morning, and workers travel down isolated dirt roads to the fields where they will spend their day constantly stooping over to fill endless tomato buckets or climbing 18-foot ladders to pluck oranges and grapefruits from the trees. Letty is part of this world. Every day after school she goes home to take care of younger brothers and sisters while her parents work the fields. When she gets a little older, she will join them, since an extra pair of hands means more family income.

Unbeknown to many teachers, Letty is honing both her survival and academic skills: mathematics (How many buckets of tomatoes does it take to buy a video game?), agriculture (Which tomatoes do you keep? Which ones do you throw away?), and life skills (How do you take care of a little sister?). Home is the migrant camp of rows and rows of cinderblock houses, one room deep, either unpainted or painted in muted tones of blue and orange. During the day, Letty's youngest sister stays at the Head Start Daycare Center, its four walls filled with colorful posters, toys, books, and children's laughter. The vacant building next door once housed a community center where people could learn English and computers skills, but cuts in funding closed its door.

Miles from the migrant camp in this vast county is the Manor, a culturally diverse, low-income neighborhood that is home to many Dolphin students. Full-size bronze sculptures of stallions rearing on their haunches mark the entrance to the Landon Country Club, one of the oldest private golf resorts in the area, on the way to the Manor. The main street of the Manor, in contrast, is lined with very small, brilliantly painted stucco houses—red, pink, and ochre—that Haitian families have built. New clapboard houses built by Habitat for Humanity line an adjacent street. Marbella and her family recently learned that they qualify for a new Habitat home, and she can't wait to have a room of her own. The Manor has grown in size and stability during the past few years because of strong cooperation between Dolphin, a nearby high school, and county community services. Lewanda Smith, director of Dolphin's Welcome Center for new immigrant students, lives in the Manor. "I *love* living in the Manor. I see the students who live there every day and I get to know them. They are my friends."

Stan and Terry represent other variations of students—the very large group of students with identified disabilities who attend the school. Twenty-three percent of Dolphin's students have identified disabilities that range from learning disabled (LD) to emotionally handicapped (EH) to varying exceptionalities (VE), including deafness. Dolphin has a higher percentage of students with disabilities than the county as a whole because parents across the county know its reputation for successfully including students with disabilities in general classrooms. A number of Manlo Island families with children with disabilities have returned to Dolphin because the services and support at Dolphin surpass what they can get in the new charter school. Eighteen percent of Dolphin students are classified as at-risk or dropout prevention students. They tend to be older students who have failed or are at risk of failing.

Faculty

The founding teachers are mainly young and almost exclusively White, with 5 years or less of teaching experience. The one Black teacher teaches mathematics, including teaching the ESOL mathematics classes. The one Latina teacher, Lisa Mendes, is a Title I teacher in charge of the Welcome Center for newly immigrated students who do not speak any English. Many members of the teaching staff have moved recently to Florida, attracted by the growth, the climate, and a keen interest in teaching. These founding teachers were excited to have a role in designing a new school. While most of these teachers are young, several are second-career teachers, who came into middle-grades teaching from business or industry with practical skills and an interest in working with young adolescents. Most of these second-career teachers worked out for the school; one was not comfortable in the classroom and was counseled out by the principal.

Dolphin Parents

Because Dolphin parents are spread over a large area in neighborhood pockets, and many lack easy transportation and time to visit the school, communication between parents and teachers is a perpetual challenge. The school works on this challenge in many ways. Posters, philosophy statements, parent newsletters, and other communication vehicles are written in English, Spanish, and Haitian Creole. During open houses and special events, parents have simultaneous broadcasts of evening meetings through headphones that translate into the three languages. Terry's father, who speaks Haitian Creole, compares all-school events to the United Nations: "They [parents] put the headphones on, and the speaker speaks one time. Everybody understands, just like the UN—they say it one time, and all the languages [English, Spanish, and Creole] are understood at the same time." The principal and teachers go out to the migrant camp and other low-income neighborhoods to meet with parents. "If parents don't have the child care and transportation to come to the school, we need to go to them," says David Piano, the school's founding principal. Hallway signs such as "Diversity Drive," "Ave. of the Americas," "Equality Lane," and "Unity Through Diversity" reflect the school's strong belief in the value and benefits of diversity. With the help of the art teacher, students painted a mural in the cafeteria that reflects their cultural backgrounds, languages, and experiences.

Standardized Test Results

Every year, Dolphin students take several statewide assessments based on state standards, including a Comprehensive Assessment Test in reading and mathematics. These test results are reported in terms of five achievement levels: Level 1 indicates little success with the challenging content. Level 3 indicates success with many of the questions but less success with the most challenging ones. Level 5 indicates success with all the questions, even the most challenging. Students also take a yearly test of expository and persuasive writing for which a passing score is 3 or better. In addition, they take the Stanford 9. Limited English proficient (LEP) students such as Marbella are required to take all of these assessments, unless they have been receiving services for less than 1 year, and even then the assessments are required if the majority of a student's LEP committee determines that the student is ready. ESE students like Terry and Stan who have a current individual education plan can take the test with appropriate modifications.

Despite the loss of most of its White, affluent students to a charter school in 1998 and an increase of migrant students and Hispanic immigrant students, Dolphin Middle School has maintained its statewide testing scores and consistently outperforms a comparable school in the district. The Florida Department of Education issues a yearly report card to every school in the state, with grades determined by the school's performance on the state assessments. Since 2000, Dolphin Middle School consistently has received a C; its "sister" school, a D. No doubt, Dolphin students have a way to go.

In 2001–02, 71% of eighth graders scored a Level 2 or better in reading; 70% scored a Level 2 or better in mathematics. Thirty-four percent of students with disabilities scored a Level 2 or better on the reading test; 40% scored a Level 2 or better on the mathematics test. In 2002–03, the scores dipped, with 55% of eighth graders scoring a Level 2 or better in reading and 32% scoring a Level 2 or better in math. Both reading and math continue to be a challenge for the school, and in 2002–03 Miner County assigned reading coaches to several schools, including Dolphin.

Writing is an area of strength for Dolphin students. They do well in part because the state focuses on highly structured forms of essays, which the school directly teaches to students. A typical task is that students are given a topic and asked to write a five-paragraph essay in which the first paragraph introduces the topic and a major idea, the next three paragraphs each develop a point or argument in support of the idea, and the fifth paragraph summarizes and concludes. The percentage of student who scored at Level 3 (passing) or better on this task increased from 76% in 1998 to 92% in 1999. The success of Black and Hispanic students doubled the number of students scoring a Level 3 or better. In 2002–03, 82% of Dolphin students scored a Level 3 or better on the writing test.

Students' Sense of Safety and Belonging

Despite the great differences in culture, family history, and place of residence in the county, Dolphin students express a sense of belonging to the school and of being valued in the school. A 1999 survey of student, teachers, and parents by the Beacons of Excellence Project showed that virtually all of the students (91%) felt that school was a "safe place." The parents agreed (95%). But 36% of the students said, when asked the question on a more personal level, that they do not feel safe in school "about half the time" or "all or most of the time." A small group of students say they sometimes worry about getting beaten up or feel picked on because of their race (12% for both of these items). A majority of students (75%) and a vast majority of parents (91%) agree that students feel they belong in the school. Similarly, both students and parents think that students are supported in their school work; they get the extra help that they need. Students and parents think that students are treated fairly in school (see Figure 2.2).

Respect is an important issue for Dolphin's diverse student body. Almost all students (87%) reported that teachers care about students and respect their families. The percentages were high across the three racial subgroups (100% for Blacks; 93% for Whites; 94% for Hispanics) and 94% of all families agreed. When we looked at their responses by race, we found that 100% of Black families, 95% of Caucasian families, and 96% of Hispanic families felt "respected by the teachers and staff at the school." They felt welcomed at the school and found that the school encouraged their involvement in school events.

CORE BELIEFS BEHIND CO-TEACHING

Dolphin's mission statement reflects the school's educational philosophy.

Dolphin's mission is to provide each student with the opportunity to obtain intellectual development consistent with the student's highest abilities. This will be accomplished by providing well-trained professional staff who hold high expectations for their own performance and whose behaviors reflect their belief that all students can learn.

Figure 2.2. Students' and Parents' Sense of Safety and Belonging

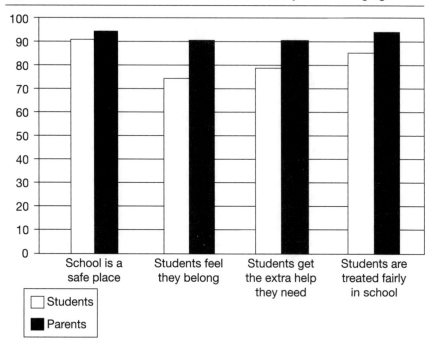

Additionally, it is our mission to maintain an environment which is academically focused, safe, orderly, and positive, and where success is recognized and celebrated. Our mission is to form a mutual commitment to academic excellence and creativity among school, home, and the community by promoting individuality, self-esteem, and wellness.

Co-teaching is Dolphin's strategy for living this mission statement. Co-teaching reflects a deeply held set of beliefs about how students learn. The beliefs are a result of the school leaders' and founding teachers' struggle to bring together the best thinking about middle-grades education for students, particularly students whose families are new Americans and who are working to obtain an economic foothold. Dolphin's core beliefs include the following:

- *A safe and caring environment.* Students learn challenging content in environments that build a sense of safety and belonging.
- *Multiple ways of learning.* Students learn in different ways and need multiple opportunities to grasp challenging content.

- *Adult collaboration.* Adults need to work closely together in order to create a personalized and academically rigorous learning environment.

Safe and Caring Learning Environment

Lewanda Smith's classroom has a soft sofa with colorful fabric pillows and a small lamp that sheds a gentle light. Pictures of her family and families of her students are framed on the wall and on tables. You could be in a family living room somewhere in Latin America or the Caribbean. At the core of the Dolphin vision is the idea that all students need to feel a sense of safety and belonging in order to be successful learners.

Research supports the philosophy that students are likely to be more academically successful when they feel safe in school. In safe learning environments, teachers understand how to interpret difficult behavior on the part of students, and they help students manage their behavior (McKinney, Montague, & Hocutt, 1998). Teachers, students, and parents use language of respect, and students learn how to interact and work with peers with different backgrounds and strengths. Students feel safer where they know what is expected of them and get frequent feedback on how they are doing, and when they feel that at least one adult knows them well (Cushman, 1990b). Tied closely to creating a sense of belonging and safety is the concept of absence of threat. When a person feels afraid and threatened, the brain "shuts down" or is too preoccupied to take in new concepts or engage in high-order thinking (Caine & Caine, 1994; Sapolsky, 1998).

Dolphin parents, students, and teachers frequently use words like "family," "caring," and "respect" when talking about the school. Piano, the founding principal, instilled in his teachers and staff the importance of what he calls the "nurturing factor"—when students feel that someone is there to care for them whom they can count on when things are not going their way. Piano elaborates on this concept:

> There is a component to middle schools that deals with the affective domain—basically how kids feel about themselves, how they interact with each other, and how they interact with adults. So much of a school is built on school climate, and if you don't have good school climate where students feel that they belong, then you really don't have good learning going on.

In talking about how he and Headley greet students at the door, Marcus explains, "You want them to feel welcome as they come in, not threatened. For them to learn, they have to feel comfortable and safe with you."

Multiple Ways of Learning

The Dolphin staff believes that all students can learn when instruction is responsive to the variety of "intelligences" and related ways of learning that students bring to the classroom. The riddling activity described earlier reflects the school's emphasis on weaving different kinds of learning within a single cooperative activity. Students use their linguistic intelligence to recall information from their reading, to attend to spelling of world leaders' names, and, certainly, to structure information as a riddle. But teachers also encourage students to visualize the settings and peoples they are writing about in connecting factual information into riddles. In Dolphin's mathematics classes, students often manipulate physical materials to help them see mathematical relationships. Teachers share the view, supported by research (Caine & Caine, 1994; Gardner, 1999), that a classroom that provides an array of different kinds of learning—opportunities to use physical and visual, as well as verbal, ways to work with and represent concepts—has more academically successful students. While Dolphin teachers do not emphasize culturally different ways of learning, they believe that all students have unique profiles of strengths, needs, and interests, and that teachers get to know those unique characteristics when adults and students have a chance to get to know one another.

Adult Collaboration

Classroom co-teaching reflects a pervasive belief that adults need to collaborate in the intellectual activities of teaching, including planning, setting up activities, problem solving, and evaluating their results with students. Behind the co-teaching observed between Marcus and Headley is a backdrop of teacher cooperation that extends beyond this lesson to a highly collaborative teaching life. The two teachers plan both together and with their team, design curricula with other teachers, and talk about student results together. Their joint work is consistent with research findings that student learning benefits when teachers examine student work together to see what students understand (Blythe, Allen, & Powell, 1999); plan curriculum units that take state standards into account (Swiderek, 1997; Tanner, 1996; Walther-Thomas, Bryant, & Land, 1996), and use assessments that help teachers and students themselves to monitor students' progress (Coben, Thomas, Sattler, & Morsink, 1997; Hobbs & Westling, 1998).

These three beliefs provide the cornerstones for the school's day-to-day life. Teachers put the beliefs into practice through co-teaching that is embedded in the schoolwide structures of teaming and looping.

DOLPHIN'S HISTORY AND THE EMERGENCE OF CO-TEACHING

As with so many large school districts, Miner Public Schools in the early 1990s were experiencing growing pains. The county needed to build a new middle school to meet its growing student population. Dolphin Middle School began as a larger K–8 model, but in 1995 it once again felt the squeeze of increasing numbers of students and separated from Dolphin Elementary.

Piano and his administrative staff wanted Dolphin to embody the best practices and knowledge that research could offer. He and his staff made themselves students. They formed a study group with the goal of inventing a school with the best possible integration of philosophies and practices for their student population. No one reform agenda gave them everything they needed. They assembled their vision from three streams of work in the field: middle-grades reform, inclusion of students with disabilities in the general curriculum and classroom, and research on human intelligence and learning. Co-teaching, an emerging practice from the inclusion movement, helped them integrate these three strands into a coherent classroom and schoolwide approach.

Middle-Grades Reform

In reading the middle-grades reform literature, Piano and assistant principal Len Clark confirmed their own experience that young adolescents naturally like to learn collaboratively. Despite the view that they are breaking away from adults, young adolescents also need personal and caring relationships with adults. The two school leaders also heard the theme of the middle-grades reform literature that when adults work together with a consistent group of students, they can know the students better and can design more stimulating learning. They drew several structural practices from the early reform movement that would respond to the developmental needs of young adolescents: interdisciplinary teaming; looping—keeping teams with the same students over 2 years (Little & Dacus, 1999); and heterogeneous grouping and advisories that build long-term teacher–student relationships. Piano came to think that "the longer you put teachers and kids together, the better it is for kids. There's a nurturing factor there, a buy-in for both the kid and the teacher." They assigned students to "vertical houses," which included sixth-, seventh-, and eighth-grade students throughout their 3 years in the school; and within each house they formed teams for the seventh- and eighth-grade students. If students leave the school and return at a later date (often because their parents are agricultural workers), they return to their house and their team. Piano and Clark also decided they would teach students to manage their schedule without bells and organized teams around block scheduling.

Research on Learning

During the school's first year, in addition to visiting other schools, administrators and teachers met with outside consultants and talked about their vision for the school. With funding from a state Break the Mold grant, the principal chose to bring in a consultant who trained teachers in practices drawn from research on how people learn. Discoveries in neuroscience and further developments in cognitive psychology gave school leaders ways to think about classroom environments for very diverse groups of students. One popular interpretation of this research that appealed to the Dolphin founders was Howard Gardner's (1999) theory of multiple intelligences, which presents a vision of seven intelligences (linguistic, logical-mathematical, spatial, bodily-kinesthetic, musical, interpersonal, and intrapersonal) that humans exhibit, sometimes with one or more kinds of intelligence more developed and dominant than others. Another interpretation is that students are natural, avid learners and respond to environments that provide complex and meaningful challenges (Caine & Caine, 1994).

During the planning for the school, the school leaders read, talked with other school leaders and consultants, and became clear that lessons that arouse the mind's search for meaning (through thematic units, for example), appeal to a variety of learning styles, help learners connect with previous experience, and encourage talk about learning are most likely to be effective. The principal recommended that teachers use integrated thematic learning and instructional practices that make difficult concepts accessible to students through different modalities, such as visual, verbal, and kinesthetic. The consultant met with the founding faculty to demonstrate these practices.

Including Students with Disabilities

Bringing students with disabilities into the regular classroom was a new idea for Miner County in the mid-1990s, requiring a strong vision and the persistence of the school's founders. "I would say, jump in with both feet, because that's what we did. We opened up [the school] with the mindset that inclusion is the best way to service special education students. Then we worked through the problems that arose," says founding assistant principal Clark, a special educator by training. "The biggest mistake you can make is assuming that conflict is a sign of dysfunction within the organization. It's just the opposite; it's a sign that people are trying new things."

Clark insisted that a well-designed middle school model would be good for students with disabilities. He also knew, however, that these students would not just slide into regular classrooms, because at that time most students with disabilities were spending all of grade school in separate classrooms and never had a sense of belonging with typical learners. "Our biggest problem was that these kids had been isolated for so long, they really didn't know how to function as students in a basic education classroom," says Clark.

Realizing they had a lot to learn about bringing students with disabilities into heterogeneous classrooms, Piano and Clark read research on teaching practices that support students with disabilities in the general education curriculum, especially students who, in addition to having disabilities, are also second-language learners, new immigrants, or children of agricultural workers (Janney, Snell, Beers, & Raynes, 1995).

Evolution of a Co-Teaching Model

One of the teaching practices emerging in the new inclusion literature was collaboration between the special education teacher and general education teacher in regular classrooms that include students with at least mild to moderate disabilities (Vaughn, Schumm, & Arguelles, 1997). Co-teaching became the integrating practice for Dolphin. It brings together teaming, inclusion, and research on learning by putting general and special education teachers together in teams that extend their work into the classroom and help all of the students engage in active and challenging learning. The principal involved his first group of faculty in thinking through a co-teaching model. The model evolved through three formats between 1995 and 1997: a collaborative model, a "traveling teacher" model, and a school-wide model.

Collaborative model. In this model, a number of "inclusion" classrooms are set up with 10 general education students, 10 special education students, and two teachers. Each inclusion class is a self-contained unit without any particular contact with other teachers and classrooms. This model, instituted in several classrooms and funded in 1995–96 by a county grant, was the first way co-teaching was implemented at the new school. Co-teaching was limited to helping students in these classrooms; the only teachers that had to think about teaching students with disabilities were the few that taught these inclusion classes.

Traveling teacher model. In this model, the special education teacher "travels," following a cohort of students with disabilities from one classroom to another to provide services to those students. The special education teacher is not a member of any team and focuses almost solely on the needs of whatever group of students with disabilities is placed in a classroom. The school shifted to this model in 1996–97, when county funds were no longer available for inclusion classes. The principal asked teams to volunteer to include students with disabilities in their classrooms and to work with a special education teacher. When the volunteer teams realized that the special education teacher knew practices of value for all of their students, they moved toward including the teacher as a member of the team.

Schoolwide model. This model, which became the Dolphin signature practice, places students with disabilities in heterogeneous classrooms within every team, with the special education teacher as a core team member. In 1997–98 this became the schoolwide approach. Tina Samuels, a special education teacher who later became dean of students, describes this period as a paradigm shift for the school.

> The first year, I began in a self-contained classroom. Toward the end of the year, I was approached about joining the sixth-grade team. It would be the first time that we really tried a true team concept with an inclusion model. They sent us out to visit local and other middle schools in the state. It was very exciting to talk to other people. [The principal] gave us the chance to create something incredible.

The model made Samuels's status as a special education teacher equal to that of the content-area teachers and made the interdisciplinary team, rather than the special education team, her primary reference group. "We began to see the buy-in of regular education teachers and exceptional education teachers that this was not only benefiting special students, but also benefiting every student in the school," Samuels recalls.

Co-teaching became the expression of interdisciplinary teaming in the classroom—a marriage of the general education teachers' content knowledge and content pedagogy and the special education teachers' strategies for making that content accessible to all students. The special education teachers carved their own niche in the teams, drawing on their expertise in understanding and responding to both students' and teachers' needs. Briana, another special education teacher, describes the role she and her colleagues play.

> In an inclusion or co-teaching model, we have to consider not only our students' needs, but also the regular education

teachers' needs. We're entering their environment and we have to be the ones to go one step above and beyond. I'm the bridge, not only between the students and the services that they need, but also between the teachers and their content areas.

According to the current deans of students, both co-teaching pioneers, this schoolwide model called for the special education teacher to plan with the entire team and then teach with each teacher in the classroom for some part of the week. Over time, decisions about how to distribute the special education teacher's co-teaching role across the content areas would depend on the needs of both the students and each particular teacher. At a minimum, the special education teacher has three roles: (1) to serve as a substantive teacher in classrooms that include students with disabilities, (2) to understand these students' learning strengths and needs, and (3) to model for the content teacher ways to make complex content accessible to a wide range of students.

MAKING CO-TEACHING WORK FOR ALL

Dolphin's signature practice—co-teaching between the general education teacher and the special education teacher—is designed to be a flexible, adaptable instructional approach that helps all students, and particularly students like Terry, Stan, Marbella, and Letty, to be successful learners. Their success on standards-based assessments depends on their having access to a standards-based, high-quality, challenging curriculum, and co-teaching is designed to provide that access.

A number of features of co-teaching at Dolphin further contribute to its coherence and, probably, to its impact in this school. The most important of these is interdisciplinary teaming, because it spreads the responsibility for teaching students with disabilities and other struggling learners to all faculty members. Other features also help co-teaching fulfill this role, including parity and flexibility in the roles of the two teachers; joint professional development for general and special education teachers; schoolwide classroom routines that build safety and belonging; a "personal best" curriculum to further motivate students; and a safety net of individual and family services (Morocco & Aguilar, 2002).

Interdisciplinary Teaming as the Context

"We have to nominate kids for the Wall of Fame today and figure out why our unit design is so confusing. And we have one hour!" Tina Samuels is the team leader for the Marlins this year, whose faculty includes five teachers—special education, language arts, science, mathematics, and social studies. Her role is not only to help the team make decisions about day-to-day business details, but also to engage them in conversations about how to support students with learning challenges participate in and be successful in the school's curriculum. She asks the team for ideas, "Carl [the science teacher] and I could use some suggestions for the lesson on tectonic plates we're teaching tomorrow. It is exciting stuff, but it's also hard for a lot of the kids."

Interdisciplinary teams have dedicated time to meet, plan, and talk about individual students. They tend to know what is going on with their students academically and personally because they stay with a group of students for 2 years and they are the point of contact for those students' parents. If a discipline problem arises, it goes straight to the team, and only if the problem persists or requires more resources does the team refer the student to a dean. Each team makes important decisions regarding scheduling and has control over a small discretionary budget for trips and supplies. Teams discuss curriculum and how best to support all students. This team milieu stands in stark contrast to what happens in many schools, where the "two silos" of special education and general education exist separately and independently from each other.

The placement of the special education teacher as a full-time team member, always present at planning meetings, enables teachers to pair strategically for the benefit of students. Team members negotiate how and where to best use co-teaching. Carl White's need for help in teaching a difficult science unit on tectonic plates can surface in team meetings without White's feeling singled out or inadequate. In the meeting snapshot above, Tina Samuels helps White save face by communicating that she herself isn't certain how best to teach complex concepts like tectonic plate movement and would appreciate suggestions from teammates.

Further, teams use their weekly planning time to share their lessons and discuss the cognitive complexities of the curriculum that students might face. This conversation determines how they will work together. Samuels, the Marlins' special education teacher, may choose to co-teach with Sam Marcus in his geography class, as we saw in the vignette that opens this chapter, or with White in his science class. The team members make the decision based on students' academic and instructional needs, and their own need to learn inclusive teaching strategies. Prior to the lesson we saw in the opening vignette, co-teachers Marcus and Headley discussed what difficulties students might have in putting together a set of clues that didn't immediately give away the riddle. They also talked about the kinds of visuals or graphic organizers that would be needed to make the ideas clear to students who have difficulty recalling and organizing information.

Parity and Flexibility in Co-Teaching Roles

"Look at the coastline of Brazil and now look at Africa. Imagine that they fit together once, until vast tectonic plates far under the ocean shifted and moved them far apart." Students are sitting in formal rows to watch a sophisticated PowerPoint presentation on plate tectonics and the formation and movement of the continents over the Earth's crust. Carl White, the science teacher, is sitting at his desk showing the slides and talking continuously, without glancing out at the blank faces in front of him. "Dr. Alfred Vegner [the teacher projects a man's image] is the scientist who is responsible for modern plate tectonics theory."

White remains at the projector, well behind his desk, showing slides of South America and Africa at different points in their formation as continents. He uses a lecture style throughout, providing very little explanation for technical concepts, and he hardly interacts with the students. As he talks, Samuels positions herself between two rows of desks, halfway between the front and back of the row, listening to the lecture while watching students' faces for signs of engagement and confusion.

White lectures on about evidence that the continents were once a single piece of land and would fit together like pieces of a jigsaw if you could put them together, and how semiliquid areas under the Earth's crust enable the crust to move. Apparently concerned that some students might not grasp all of this, Samuels intervenes with a metaphor. "I'm trying to think what to compare this to." She turns around to face the class then spreads out her arms dramatically. "It's like a *surfboard*. The ocean is like the lithosphere [the semiliquid matter under the Earth's crust], it moves the surfboard, and me sitting on the surfboard is like the continents." She walks to the board and draws a surfer "hanging ten." A student comments, "Like a bearing. The lithosphere. Things move on it." "Yes!" Samuels says, pleased.

The class becomes a "duo-lecture" as White shows the slides and Samuels asks questions and explains ideas related to plate tectonics theory. Her questions prompt students to use their background knowledge and experience to build understanding. White is well aware that his teaching goes over many students' heads, but he's not certain what to do about it. In the context of co-planning, co-teaching, and intervening to help students understand, Samuels also is demonstrating to White some ways to make science content more accessible to all of their students.

Samuels does not always use this approach in her co-teaching role. Sometimes she takes on the lead role; other times she "team teaches," as Headley and Marcus do in the opening riddling scene; sometimes she mainly works with individual students. Figure 2.3 shows the range of instructional roles that both the general education and special education

Figure 2.3. Teaching Roles and Strategies for General and Special Education Teachers

Teaching Role	Strategies
Set up/engage students in learning experience	Teachers prepare students for a learning opportunity by (a) explaining the activity, (b) clarifying directions, (c) providing examples of how to carry out the activity, and/or (d) modeling how a student might participate in the activity.
Motivate learning	Teachers engage students in the activity by (a) requesting or encouraging their participation in an activity and/or (b) providing specific incentives for participation.
Provide instruction	Teachers directly provide or guide content-area learning by (a) providing information, (b) explaining concepts, (c) posing questions, (d) responding to students' questions, (e) re-voicing responses, (f) modeling learning strategies, and/or (g) using visual or graphic support.
Monitor/provide feedback on work	Teachers guide students' work by (a) giving praise/reinforcement, (b) giving negative or constructive feedback, (c) examining students' work, and/or (d) suggesting specific changes.
Manage instruction and behavior	Teachers organize students' work by (a) guiding collaboration, (b) distributing/collecting materials, (c) managing transitions, (d) managing time, and/or (e) evaluating behavior.
Assist individual students	Teachers help students manage and progress in their work by (a) circulating to observe students at work, (b) coaching individual students, and/or (c) coaching small groups of students.
Confer with co-teacher	Co-teachers audibly converse about the direction of the lesson.

teachers may take in Dolphin. In the scene above, both are presenting instruction, but while White simply is presenting information, Samuels is helping students understand it by posing questions, explaining concepts, and using visual metaphors.

What is unusual in this school is that both teachers take all of these roles at some point. Overall, they do, however, distribute their "moves" across these teaching roles somewhat differently. As Figure 2.4 shows, the general education teachers do more instructing, and the special education teachers do more monitoring of how students are doing and give more individual help (Morocco & Aguilar, 2002). Although highly experienced co-teachers like Marcus and Headley both use a broad range of strategies, Marcus admits that Headley is the one who really "brings an expertise with the different styles of teaching like mind-maps, charts, and webs to record student thinking and help them organize their thoughts."

While co-teachers try to be flexible in exactly what roles they take within the same teaching pair and lesson, this does not always happen. With the science teacher, White, Samuels was able to interrupt the flow with her own strategies to make the ideas more accessible. By comparison, her co-teaching with the language arts teacher looked surprisingly like the traditional special education teacher aide role. The language arts teacher was uncomfortable with having students with disabilities in the classroom and working with a co-teacher. The principal encouraged the teacher to relocate to a different school, and she left before the end of the year.

Figure 2.4. Roles in Co-Teaching

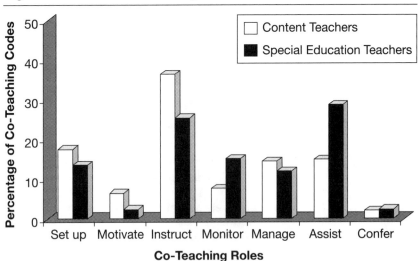

Joint Professional Development

Co-teaching within inclusive interdisciplinary teaming not only brings special education expertise, particularly knowledge of inclusive strategies, to the content teacher; it also brings content knowledge to the special education teacher. While Samuels has a fairly strong science and mathematics background, she has less experience with history and language arts. Headley, in contrast, has strong social science and language arts skills, but less knowledge of mathematics and science. Their goals are to absorb enough content to give students substantive coaching during co-teaching. It helps that they are part of curriculum design sessions and plan co-teaching lessons.

Joint professional development extends the opportunities for general and special education teachers to learn from one another and for both to improve their content and strategic knowledge. In many schools, content teachers have separate professional development experiences from those of special education teachers. At Dolphin, when a consultant comes to help deepen the understanding of varied learning styles, all teachers participate and nonteaching staff may participate as well. The entire staff of the school was present, for example, when a consultant presented a common framework and a set of schoolwide practices for creating a sense of belonging on the part of a culturally and academically diverse group of students. The staff worked on how to meet the needs of diverse learners from the time they step on the bus, throughout their classes, to the time they step back off the bus at the end of the day.

Schoolwide Classroom Routines

"Hi, Terry. How's the student council dance going?" When students walk into Marcus's classroom, he and Headley stand ready to greet them at the door, chatting briefly with each one. Marcus asks Terry about a dance, knowing that the boy recently lost the student council presidential election by a narrow margin. These routines support co-teaching by extending teacher support to students' point of entry into and exit from the classroom. Teachers try to foster a sense of belonging by creating an environment where students feel teachers care about them and feel secure in their knowledge of classroom expectations. Marcus says, "It's a discipline thing. It's a very subtle thing, but when they walk into the room, they know that they are coming in, and there are certain expectations and behaviors that I demand from them. For them to learn, it has to be a very safe environment and that little subtlety makes it very nice. If you pay attention to the details of what is going on with them, you avoid these gigantic blowouts because you can pick up that a child is having a bad day."

Marcus and Headley structure their daily activities to include posting daily agendas, fine tuning seating arrangements, and staying on top of classroom norms. Teachers settle students down with a quieting routine: "Counting down . . . 5, 4, 3, 2, 1." Throughout this time, students usually are retrieving their books and other materials. Next, a start-up activity "warms up the students' brains," as the teachers put it, through problem solving and creative thinking. Often the problems are samples of the kinds of writing activities or subject-area questions they will get on the statewide tests. These routines help Stan, a student with autism who tends to be highly distractible, focus on what is immediately in front of him.

A Personal Best Curriculum

Hand in hand with middle-grades students' academic growth come their social and emotional needs. Dolphin co-teachers specifically target students' social developmental learning through a character curriculum called Life Skills that gives them a common language for thinking and talking about how to behave responsibly in a learning community. At the beginning of each year, the faculty and students set aside time to talk about concepts such as integrity, initiative, effort, and responsibility. A bright poster in the library splashes the word "trustworthiness" on a colorful background. Similar posters in the library, inside hallways, and classrooms advertise truthfulness, active listening, "no put-downs!" and personal best. Announcements on the daily student-run news broadcast and classroom conversations provide constant, explicit reminders that these rules for life guide everyday interactions in Dolphin.

Stan says that Life Skills is important "because it teaches us to care and everything. Every teacher has it in her classroom. It teaches kids not to be putting down people. It's just really good, and I like it." Letty describes a street sign on one of the outside walkways that says "Perseverance": "It's down my science class wing. It's just showing another life skill. We have Life Skills street signs all over the place." Asked what the sign means, she says, "It means that you can do something if you work hard enough."

Teachers use some team meeting time to come up with ways to bring these concepts alive in the classroom. Marcus and Headley pepper their interactions with their students with this language of respect. They thank their students for getting ready to learn and compliment them on their promptness: "Thank you for listening," "I appreciate the way every desk is cleared off," "It's a pretty good feeling when you know you got them [answers] right, isn't it?" "Good notebook order. I appreciate that." Their consistent and detailed attention to students' behavior keeps the life skills curriculum concrete.

A Safety Net of Services

Co-teaching works for all students because teachers attend to personal and family problems that might keep students from being ready to learn. Teachers do this through schoolwide programs such as mentoring, the Safe Core team, conflict mediation, and forums with families.

Mentor in the middle. Support for students is embedded in the teams and extends out to the community. One teacher from every team is designated as a "Mentor in the Middle," someone who will listen to students in confidence without passing judgment and who will help them think through their problems. Using dropout money, the principal frees up a teacher from each team to work with students who are experiencing behavior, attendance, or grade problems. He describes the mentors' role as largely preventive and oriented to strengthening the teams.

> They work with their fellow teammates in terms of what has been successful with Johnny and Mary, who are potential for dropout, and then they work with the team to design individual behavior plans for the students. The team identifies things the student can do to enhance his academics. What we try to do with that program is find kids *doing things right*, rather than wrong, so we're being proactive with not only the academic success but also with the discipline.

The school is laced with programs that try to catch students before they fall. In addition to Mentor in the Middle, Dolphin has a peer mediation program, a Safe Core connection with community services, and informal ways of getting to the families that are scattered, some at considerable distance, across many neighborhoods.

Safe core. "SAFE CORE TEACHERS LISTEN AND HELP." This sign is highly visible on Sam Marcus's classroom window that looks out onto a walkway. The sign tells students that Marcus is on the Safe Core team, a schoolwide committee of teachers and counselors who work with community agencies to make referrals for students who are demonstrating problems. The assistant principal summarizes the role of the group.

If you are really having some disruptive behaviors showing up in the classroom or out here on campus, why is that happening? Is there some other agency that we can involve to help? That has proven very effective as well because we have been able to get outside agencies involved. The Safe Core committee meets once a month; teams come forward with names, and it just doesn't stop there.

Conflict mediation. Counselors train all sixth graders in conflict mediation, "so that students know that there is somebody here who cares; somebody here who listens; there's a process for it, and they are going to have a lot of say as a student, and the teachers are going to have a lot of ways as a team in terms of how things are done," in the words of Piano. Discipline referrals have dropped from over 800 in the first year of the conflict mediation program to under 100 in the third year. Piano says, "We know the system works, and it works quite successfully in a very diverse student population."

Forums with families. Piano and his staff visit and work with families who live in the Manor and migrant camps. They sponsor forums in the different communities to talk directly with parents about what is happening in the school. When Piano goes out to a migrant camp, he meets with parents in the day care center. He makes a point of running into parents outside of school and chatting with them whenever possible. Terry's mother remembers when she encountered Piano at the local grocery store where she worked.

> When I was going through a divorce and both my sons were going to school at Dolphin, the principal came up to me and said if the boys were having any problems, I could talk to the counselors. He reminded me that I could get help if they needed it because of the family situation. They never had any problems, but he was right on it like that with me.

Co-Teaching Challenges for Teachers

Working as a team does not come easily; personalities sometimes can get in the way. Dolphin co-teachers like to compare co-teaching with a marriage where they know one another so well that they "complete one another's sentences." When disagreements occur, teachers need to discuss the problem and continue. In some cases, the teams are reconfigured. But for the most part, the team's "esprit de corps" helps members through the hurdles that they encounter in meeting the demands of all of their students. Their hurdles include many that other middle-grades teachers face on a daily basis: not enough time in the day, curriculum demands, large class sizes, grading papers, and district mandates, to name a few.

Teachers also worry that even with two teachers in the classroom to support the most vulnerable students, not every student's needs will be met. The great emphasis on leveling the playing field for the struggling learners may mean that sometimes the capable students do not get the stimulation and challenge that they need. For example, Arnold, an eighth-grade African American general education student, does very well in his classes and probably could stretch to greater challenges. When the research team shadowed Arnold for a day, we found that in class after class he understood the concepts being taught (such as map coordinates, ordered pairs of numbers, and number sequences in math class) and actively participated in answering questions. He did not seem to have difficulty in understanding the big ideas, always had all of his materials organized, and was ready for class with a minimum of fuss and bother.

But rather than being provided additional challenges, Arnold often was drafted to assist other students. He often took on the role of the group leader, keeping his group focused and helping members find the right books and materials. Tutoring has been found to benefit the tutor as well as the tutee (Vaughn, Gersten, & Chard, 2000); but for the very able student, it may not fully substitute for advanced challenges. A project researcher writes in her field notes, "I never saw Arnold challenged in any meaningful way. He was never asked a question that demanded higher order thinking skills, nor did he participate in any meaningful discussion around language or geography. Arnold had an okay day because he worked hard at whatever was given to him and mostly maintained his own motivation."

By extending collaboration from the interdisciplinary team to the co-teachers and the student helpers, the school strains to provide its most challenged students with academic support. In the process, this informal tutoring, without other kinds of academic stretch for the tutor, may under-challenge the very able students.

LEADERSHIP CHALLENGES AND CHANGES

Looking back on his time at Dolphin, the principal says, "The hardest thing we had to do in the last 6 years was get this thing up and running, because we had to fight the static conditions within the system. What I wanted to do was a little bit different. It was kind of like the nail that's stuck up and everybody was trying to hammer me down." Although Dolphin could be viewed as a school that is not academically stellar, somewhat "behind the curve," Piano and his staff based Dolphin on a foundation of research-based practices to support all learners that put it ahead of the curve in his district in taking on middle school reforms and inclusive practices. From the beginning, organizing the school was a challenge. Maintaining Dolphin's inclusive schoolwide culture and co-teaching practice is an ongoing job for Piano and his administrative staff. No one questions Piano's commitment to his integrated model of middle-grades structures, inclusion, and instruction based on research. The decision-making powers he gives to teams, common planning time, and team autonomy are all a message to teachers that he trusts their collective judgment.

Staffing

The challenges to co-teaching and Dolphin's inclusive culture have less to do with commitment to the core beliefs of the school than with the school's *capacity* to continue Piano's vision into the new millennium. The most critical area of capacity for Dolphin is *staffing*. Several challenges related to the faculty could erode the school's signature practice and the interdisciplinary teaming context for that practice. One challenge is staff turnover and preparation for co-teaching. A core of pioneer teachers, including Samuels, Marcus, Headley, White, and others, has deep experience in working as a team and collaborating to co-teach. But yearly staff changes are increasing, and new teams may have a lot to learn. One danger is that in having considerable autonomy, teams may focus on their students and houses to the exclusion of bigger schoolwide needs and changes, such as acculturating a new crop of teachers across the school as a whole. If staff turnover increases, the teachers who helped develop the model may need additional incentives and time carved out for them to support new teachers and help acculturate new teams.

Teachers' Cultural Awareness

Another challenge, related to teacher turnover, is teachers' increasing need for training that focuses directly on cultural diversity. The school has two teachers of color—Page Carver, an African American math teacher, and Lisa Mendez, a Latina teacher in charge of the Welcome Room. The cultural gap between staff and students is wide, and there has been no system in place to support teachers' learning about their students' cultures and backgrounds. In 2001, the research team returned to visit the school and met a first-year teacher from the midwest who had done her student teaching at Dolphin. She shared that throughout her training in a small college town in Ohio, she had never been prepared as a White, English-speaking teacher to work with English language learners with language, economic, and cultural backgrounds vastly different from her own. She was surprised at how thrown she was by having English language learners in her class, some of whom quickly picked up on her lack of confidence and challenged her. With time and support from her team and the ESOL teacher, she was beginning to use many of their strategies to manage her students and help them learn, and she is excited about cooperative teaching with the special education teacher on her team. Yet a large influx of new and relatively inexperienced teachers with cultural backgrounds very different from those of Dolphin students could tax the capacity of teams to socialize new staff members.

District Policies

District and state practices, policies, and mandates can strengthen or erode the school's capacity to sustain inclusive, interdisciplinary co-teaching. Each October, student enrollment determines each school's teaching allocation or full-time equivalents. For Dolphin, that cutoff date is a disadvantage because many migrant and new immigrant students return to school after mid-October, thereby increasing the total student enrollment. An increased ratio of students to teachers increases class size and reduces Piano's staffing flexibility. State policies also set 3 years as the time required for a new teacher to get tenured in Miner County. At the end of that time, a teacher can apply to any of the other schools in the district, and many do. Why? Schools that perform well in the state assessments receive an A rating and are financially rewarded by the state. Teachers receive a bonus ranging from $1,000 to $1,500. Thus, many of the Dolphin teachers, working in a school that needs to meet the literacy and learning needs of some of the lowest-income students in the state and one of the largest migrant student populations, seek schools with higher rankings and salary incentives.

While Dolphin is not exactly a maverick school in the district, the principal has come to have a stronger following on the national middle-grades reform scene than in his own district. Piano became president of a national middle school organization as his school blossomed as an integrated model of middle-grades education. Piano maintained close connections with the district and was responsive to district demands. And the district special education director supported an inclusive school philosophy and co-teaching through staff development opportunities. The district leaders expressed the view that students with disabilities must be served in general education classes to the extent possible, given that they are included in high-stakes, standards-based tests. In the eyes of district special education leaders, Dolphin is successful in helping the district serve its most challenging student and family population. At the same time, the school's independent vision and aggressive seeking of connections with a larger reform community also made it slightly out of step with the timetable and school models within its own district.

Changes in Inclusion Resources

Changes in the groups of special education students who were being educated at Dolphin had an impact on the school leaders' time and resources. The district created a center for students with severe emotional disabilities (SED) at Dolphin, based on the number of students in need of intensive services in Dolphin's "home zone" in comparison with other zones within the large school district. Because of their IEP placement recommendations, these new students were placed in self-contained classes. This challenging population required the school administrators and special education staff to devote considerable attention to supporting the SED teachers in meeting the challenging needs of the students in these classrooms.

Still another area of capacity that is critical to sustaining co-teaching within a teaming context is funding for sufficient numbers of special education staff to make every team inclusive. Throughout the history of co-teaching in the school, Piano and Clark have managed to create a financial structure that gives priority to placing special education teachers within the teams. Continuing to embed co-teaching within interdisciplinary teams requires a constant stream of funding for these teachers.

Sustaining Leadership with Vision

The administrative team of Piano and Clark, together with the pioneering general education and special education teachers, has brought their vision and the core beliefs about education into every corner of school life. Should either or both administrators leave, the school will need new leaders who can continue to steer the current practices through new times and new demands. Piano acknowledges that "the weakest cog in any administrative program is that administrators aren't trained to build capacity within the organization. You have to have capacity *within* if you are going to sustain any kind of systemic change." Yet he thinks Dolphin has potential leaders that can sustain and continue the school without him, should he move on.

> I could leave tomorrow and this place would continue to go because I've got enough people now in place to make it hap-

pen. It's not relying on me. It's not relying on Len; it's not relying on Kevin or Sam or Tina. All of us play a part in that, but one of us could leave, and we would be able to fill that gap with somebody who's ready to take their place. I think that 6 years have built that up.

But knowing, as he does, what it has taken him to keep the school evolving within the integrated vision that he and his staff created at the founding of the school, he does voice some concern. "The real question is will those people have enough fortitude and stick-to-itiveness to fight the system to *allow* us to continue? That's the key." The real question may be whether Dolphin's inclusive model and signature practice, co-teaching, can withstand the new rounds of high-stakes testing and accountability policies that may challenge the school's vision.

Exhibitions at Leonardo Da Vinci Middle School

An original poster for the film *Grease*, with John Travolta and Olivia Newton-John, projected from a computer, covers most of one classroom wall. Karin's part of her team's PowerPoint slide presentation is underway. "This movie is about the 50s. Two teenagers are trying to keep their friendship with the T-Birds and the Pink Ladies, and also their relationship between each other." A seventh grader whose parents emigrated from Honduras before she was born, Karin is presenting her part of a group project on America in the 1950s in English at Leonard Da Vinci Middle School.

Although Spanish is her first language, Karin speaks English fluently. Her presentation is the culmination of intensive personal effort. She copes with dyslexia and perceptual impairment that make both reading and auditory processing difficult. She has been able to manage her research and preparation with help from adults and her two partners, Tomás and Javier. Both boys are typical learners without disabilities. Born in Colombia, Javier just recently transitioned from the school's bilingual program into Karin's social studies class and is less fluent in English than either of the other two presenters. Following Karin's slides on films of the 1950s, her partners talk about what they have learned about music, dance, dress, and other aspects of American popular culture.

Immediately after the presentation, which the school calls an exhibition, the students easily handle questions from the audience. Their self-confidence is palpable.

> *Adult:* Were there things going on in the 50s that we see happening today?
> *Tomás:* Some of the dances are still done. The twist, and the movie *Grease* is still being seen. The haircuts are really different, though.
> *Adult:* What have been some of the changes?

> *Karin:* Now there's more music from different countries, and
> even though we use some of the music from the 50s, we're
> changing it.
> *Adult:* Where did you get your information?
> *Javier:* Internet, especially for the pictures and posters. Since mostly
> all three of us were not born then. And my mom had records
> from her mom. And the history books we read.
> *Adult:* How did you get it all together?

Tomás explains that they got information from all of those places, then
scanned in the pictures. They went to PowerPoint, got a new slide, wrote
the most important information, went to their file of pictures, and took
pictures from Movie Scan to illustrate their points. Asked what the other
kids in the class were doing while their group of three worked on researching popular culture, Tomás responds:

> Every group had a different topic on the 50s. Mrs. D. put all of
> our slides together in one zip disc, and it's like a whole show
> going on. We were doing timelines from the 1900s to 2000, with
> the music, politics, wars. All of them together—and all of the time
> periods for music, movies, and popular stuff from 1900 to 2000!

The students and teachers at this school expect seventh graders to be
able to conduct research on a complex topic; organize and connect information; identify the important findings; and write up and present their
information and ideas to their classmates and teachers, and, periodically,
to their parents. They also expect students to use advanced technology
tools, including Internet searches, database software, word processing, and
PowerPoint, in carrying out the various stages of their work.

The regularity with which students exhibit their work in this way in
their various subject-area classes—usually once in each of the four marking periods—reveals teachers' and school leaders' expectation that students can take on intellectual challenges and master complex ideas. This
expectation extends to students with disabilities, including those with
moderate learning disabilities and cognitive delay, and students who
have recently emmigrated to the United States, including those who do
not yet speak English.

Exhibitions are a signature practice in Leonardo Da Vinci because they
are a pervasive, familiar way to learn and communicate about learning in
the school. Teachers intend that every student will get the help he or she
needs to understand this way of learning and will develop the skills to use
research and presentation tools.

School leaders first heard the idea of exhibition from the Coalition of Essential Schools, founded by Theodore Sizer at Brown University, when Da Vinci began to explore being a Coalition partner (Cushman, 1990a; McDonald, 1996; Silva & Mackin, 2002). But the school founders fashioned the approach to their own goals and needs, and to the kinds of students who attend the school—students who need many opportunities to talk, read, and write in English. Da Vinci exhibitions differ from those of the Coalition in at least three ways.

- They take place throughout the year, mainly as a form of instruction, while the Coalition uses exhibitions for end-of-year assessment and grading.
- Da Vinci students develop exhibitions in small groups, while they are mainly an individual undertaking in Coalition schools.
- Students use extensive technology resources and tools, while technology is not necessarily central in Coalition schools.

These and other distinctive features, listed in Figure 3.1, are the trademarks of exhibitions at this school, and the features work together to make this way of learning accessible to students with varied academic abilities and cultural backgrounds. A team of two to four students conducts an in-depth investigation of a topic in a content-area course and presents its results to other students, faculty, and parents, using a variety of media in PowerPoint formats. Special features of the school's exhibitions that work together to make them accessible to all students in the school include the following:

- *Technology tools* and resources help students find, organize, and present information and ideas
- *Adult scaffolding* makes exhibitions accessible to individual learners
- *Informal peer assistance* is encouraged throughout the learning process
- *Exhibitions in Spanish* support transitioning second-language learners
- *Social support*, through mentoring and peer mediation, builds collaboration
- *Teachers collaborate* to assess and improve exhibitions.

The school embraces exhibitions because they engage students in the kind of learning that teachers think is important: building background knowledge, finding information that is relevant to important topics and

Figure 3.1. Exhibitions at Leonardo Da Vinci

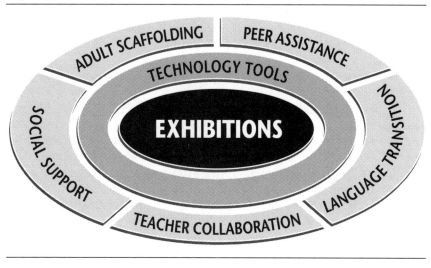

questions, identifying what is most important, and communicating ideas clearly in *English*. And the school has a deeper purpose in making exhibitions a way of learning and providing students many kinds of support to be successful. It wants students—mainly low-income Latino students, many recent immigrants acquiring English language proficiency—to be able to be successful in middle school and move on to high school. Further, the school wants them to move into the mainstream of the United States equipped with the knowledge, critical stance toward information, and informational and technology skills that are the currency of today's marketplace and employment-base.

MEET A SCHOOL FOR CHILDREN OF IMMIGRATION

Streaming toward Leonardo Da Vinci Middle School at 7:30 a.m., students jam the neighborhood sidewalks. Not a single bus or car drops them off, since almost all 360 students live within walking distance from the school. A mile long and a quarter of a mile wide, with 60,000 residents, United City is the most densely populated city in the United States. Most students live in two- or three-story multifamily homes, tightly packed along busy streets. Da Vinci, as students and faculty call the school, is overcrowded, and students share the cafeteria and gym of a Catholic school across the street. The school sits directly across the Hudson River from Manhattan's financial district. Da Vinci students witnessed the destruction of the World Trade Center from the windows of their gym.

The Students

Students reflect the "Latino tapestry" (Suarez-Orozco & Suarez-Orozco, 1995) of the city, which was a popular port of entry for Cubans in the 1960s and 70s now is home to families from Mexico, the Dominican Republic, Puerto Rico, and Central America (including El Salvador, Guatemala, and Honduras). Approximately 95% of the students in the school are Latino and 75% of them do not speak English at home. Because most of the students came from low-income Latin American communities, the vast majority are on free and reduced-price lunch. Close to 15% of the students have been in the country less than 3 years and are "children of immigration"—either they or their parents are foreign born (Suarez-Orozco & Suarez-Orozco, 2001).[1]

In a 1999 survey of students, teachers, and parents by the Beacons of Excellence Project, most students said, "I feel like I belong in this school," and a majority said, "I am proud of this school." Virtually all (95%) said that the school "is a safe place." Nevertheless, the sense of safety is not total; asked the question on a more personal level, about 36% said that they do not feel safe in school "about half the time" or "all or most of the time." The teachers think that this is partly because of typical age-related conflicts over relationships, but also because of fighting among student groups from different countries of origin—a pervasive issue and concern for faculty. (Figure 3.2 summarizes these survey results.)

Almost all students reported that teachers care about students and respect their families. Students feel supported in their work; most said, "I get the extra help in school that I need." Similar proportions of the students reported that they are treated fairly in school.

Like their peers, students with disabilities, who are potentially the most vulnerable students in the school, are positive about their personal involvement in Da Vinci. Close to 90% said they are treated fairly in school, and all reported that teachers and staff care about and respect them. As a group, they also felt that they belong in the school, with only 5% saying, "I feel like I don't know a lot of kids in the school." More than two out of every three students with disabilities believed that Da Vinci students try hard to get good grades. More than half (53%) said that most of the time students who are having problems ask a teacher for help.

Figure 3.2. Students' Sense of Safety and Belonging

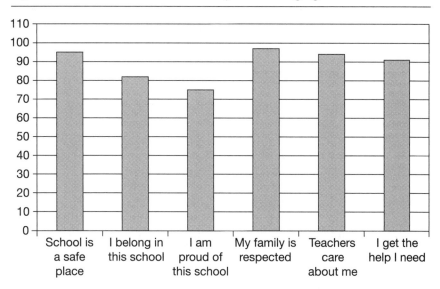

The Faculty

Over half of the Da Vinci faculty members are Latino; one is African American (a teacher who heads a program for over-age students) and the rest are White. The Latino teachers are mainly Cuban; their families were part of the early Cuban migration to United City, which for many years was known as "Little Havana." One Puerto Rican and one Cuban American teacher head the school's bilingual program and work in many ways to get the newest students acclimated to the school and ensure that assessments sort out, as much as possible, which students are struggling with disabilities as well as language proficiency. Without exception, teachers in the school are certified in English as a second language and trained in strategies to support second-language learners in every classroom.

In the Beacons survey, all of the teachers agreed that the school is a safe place. A vast majority (91%) said that students feel they belong and all said that teachers care about students. The involvement of many teachers in providing students help before and after school and on Saturdays is consistent with this expression of positive commitment. A lower percentage of teachers expressed strong satisfaction with their own teaching. While 100% of teachers felt that students get the extra help they need, a lower percentage (75%) thought that special education students' needs are met, that there is enough support for different learning styles, and that their learning approach helps students work together. One of the directors of the bilingual program says that this is because "at Da Vinci, *we never rest! If we accomplish one thing, we move on to the next.*"

Performance on Standardized Tests

Despite the many challenges that students bring to learning, Da Vinci students' academic motivation and success are palpable. In May 1998, the students had the highest overall pass rates of any school in United City on practice administrations of the Early Warning Test, a statewide pilot test. The school also had the district's best attendance rate for students and faculty for 2 years, the highest number of students transferring into the school, and the lowest number transferring out between 1993 and 1996. More students from Da Vinci qualified for the ninth-grade honors program that year than from any other city school. In 1998, the school's eighth-grade students were at the state norm in language arts literacy. From 1999 to 2001, Da Vinci eighth graders received the highest pass rate of any eighth graders in the city (with the exception of students in the gifted and talented school) on the statewide Grade 8 Proficiency Assessment (GEPA) in both reading/language arts and mathematics.

Recent scores continue to be strong. The percentage of the student body that passed the language arts GEPA was 95.6% in 2003 and 90.0% in 2004. The percentage of students who passed the mathematics GEPA was 81.1% in 2003 and rose to 91.5% in 2004. Percentages passing science were 76.7% in 2003 and 81.4% in 2004. Students with disabilities passing at the proficient level in language arts rose from 23.1% in 2003 to 37.0% in 2004; and in mathematics from 26.9% in 2003 to 40.7% in 2004. In science 36% were proficient in 2003 and 44.4% in 2004. The school's scores for eighth-grade students with disabilities are the highest in the district. While the school acknowledges that students with disabilities are making progress in passing high-stakes tests, the school has a long way to go in reaching its goals for these students.

CORE BELIEFS BEHIND EXHIBITIONS

Exhibitions reflect strongly held beliefs about how students learn and *who* can learn at Da Vinci. While faculty and school leaders do not explicitly state them, the following core ideas come across in many details of school life:

- *Intellectual competence.* Low-income students can build knowledge in the major content areas and can learn to use a range of intellectual tools to do so.
- *Cultural responsiveness.* Students learn more readily when their learning environment is responsive to their language and cultures.
- *Familial learning community.* Young adolescents and their families, and particularly Latino students, are more likely to participate fully in school when school and parents work together.

Underlying these beliefs is a commitment to having low-income Latino students acquire the knowledge, skills, and personal identities that they need in order to continue their education, advocate for themselves, and find a respected role in society.

Intellectual Competence

"These are low-income kids; people don't always expect that they can learn anything they need to. We just need to give them tools." Da Vinci teachers often talk about their students' intellectual competence, as though to defy age-old stereotypes that poor, non–English-speaking students have cognitive deficits that keep them from mastering challenging material. A strong body of research supports their belief that students disadvantaged by poverty and/or disability acquire basic skills best through instruction that motivates them to use higher level thinking to construct ideas and solve problems (Means, Chelemer, & Knapp, 1991). Research finds that when students learn skills in the context of real-world questions and problems, they also learn how and when to use those skills (Vaughn, Gersten, & Chard, 2000). For example, as they investigate their topics, students build essential reading comprehension skills in vocabulary development, selecting the main idea from a text, summarizing passages, posing and answering questions, and expressing ideas visually and in text (RAND Reading Study Group, 2002). Teachers believe that the most intellectually challenging questions do not have fixed, correct answers but are open-ended and, in students' eyes, relevant to their lives beyond school (Newmann & Associates, 1996).

Cultural Responsiveness

When the school holds schoolwide exhibitions, and invites families and community members, girls perform dances from their countries of origin that they've taught one another. But respect for students' cultures exists at a deeper level in the school than dance and cultural celebrations, which potentially can serve to exclude different groups through stereotyping (Morey & Kilano, 1997). Teachers use practices like exhibitions that assume the equality of every member of the school, give each student an active role, and help to form a cooperative rather than a competitive learning community (Delpit, 1995). The school opens up opportunities for leadership to every student; the student council averages 30 because it includes every student who signs up. In contrast with many schools where bilingual classes are given less intellectually demanding work (Nieto, 1996), second-language learners participate in the same curriculum as the general classroom students.

Exhibitions weave together many practices, such as cooperative learning and peer coaching, that are culturally responsive in that they encourage students to work with one another rather than in isolation or in competition, to take control of their learning, and to talk with one another to build ideas (Ladson-Billings, 1994, 2001). Although students acquire English proficiency as soon as possible, the school respects students' first language and culture and encourages students to make connections between their academic tasks in school and their home cultures. In contrast with current language policies in most states, Da Vinci teachers encourage students to use and develop their native language while they are becoming proficient in English. Walking through the hallways, visitors hear lively talk in Spanish and English. Teachers view language as more than a tool for communication; they see it as a way for these young adolescents to retain and carry forward connections to their original cultures while they build new identities as English-speaking Americans. The idea is that students will build full "transcultural" identities (Suarez-Orozco & Suarez-Orozco, 2001).

Familial Learning Community

The faculty believes that knowing students' families is a vibrant part of respecting and understanding the students and making them feel they belong. In general, Latino (as well as African American) students identify their parents as their greatest source of academic motivation (Noguera, 2003). Nevertheless, connecting with parents, many of whom are struggling to find work and raise children in a new and strange country, is a constant challenge for teachers and school leaders. To help families transition into the community and connect with the school, Da Vinci hired a full-time parent liaison in 1998 who is a mother of a student in the school. "I'm a bridge," she says, because she speaks, reads, and writes in both English and Spanish and gets information to families in both languages. She tries to help families find places to shop for clothes and school supplies and connects them with health facilities. She says that some newcomer parents are unaccustomed to having an active role in their child's education and her job is to "make them aware what their job is here as a parent and how they can better their child's academics."

Parents attend the school's Parent University after school and on Saturdays, where they can enhance their employability by learning English and computer skills (Word, PowerPoint, and Excel). They learn how to navigate the Web and use the Internet to look for jobs. In a gathering of parents with the school's parent liaison, a father who speaks very little English described how a job opened up for him in United City after he took two technology courses. Another father said that the courses gave him "the power to communicate with Montefiore Hospital about my headaches."

The most important way the school connects with families is through the Expo—schoolwide exhibitions that happen two or three times a year, bringing together parents, teachers, and students in the auditorium across the street to see students present what they are learning. For parents who've grown up in Latin American or Caribbean countries with formal and teacher-centered education systems, the student-led exhibitions are a novel indeed. Parents are not simply passive members of the audience; they sew costumes and help their children with research, as Javier's mother did by giving him phonograph records from the 1950s. And some parents themselves present exhibitions. When parents take a computer course in Parent University, their teachers encourage them to use their own new PowerPoint tools to display to the school community what they are learning.

Early on, the founding principal, Roger Fabio, reached out to families in a variety of ways. He developed e-mail relationships with students and their families, leading to a deeper understanding of the impact of poverty on his students' daily lives. Fabio also took an aggressive role in working with parents to get students to school. If a student was absent for more than a day, he walked to the student's home, knocked on the door, and, after speaking with the mother, might walk into a student's bedroom to wake him and tell him the school was waiting for him. He also went to students' homes to settle disputes. A television cameraman from a crew that was preparing a show on the school followed the principal to the home of a student whose "gang" had stolen a bike belonging to another student. The principal personally asked for the bike to be returned. It was.

Fabio encouraged teachers to build relationships with new families. He modeled outreach to families because it was sometimes difficult for his faculty. For example, because the largely Cuban faculty comes from a generation that gave up its identification with its first homeland when it emigrated to the United States, many teachers initially found it difficult to

understand Dominican families, who took their children out of school periodically to visit their primary home in the Dominican Republic.

Together, these varied ways of connecting with parents seem to have
an impact, for parents echo their children's sense of safety and belonging
in the school. (Figure 3.3 summarizes survey results.) Most think the school
keeps order and discipline and holds high behavioral and academic expectations for all students.

"On a day that I went to pick up my daughter at school, I was amazed
at the strong bonds teachers have with their students." A father of a family that recently came from Colombia is surprised at the relationships he
sees between his daughter, Monica, and Da Vinci teachers. In an interview
translated from Spanish, he goes on:

> The teachers are always prepared to help and protect a student.
> Monica's teacher, who she had only been with for 2 months,
> talked to me about Monica extensively, as if she had known her
> for a long time. This care gives parents assurance that their

Figure 3.3. Parents' and Teachers' Perceptions of the School

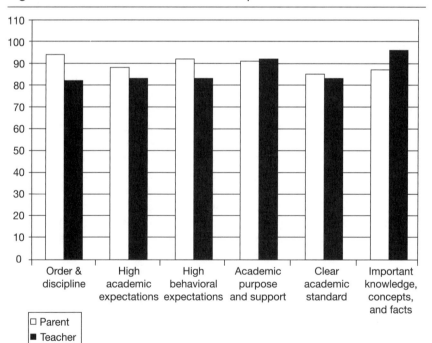

children are receiving a good education and it makes parents want to participate.

Monica's father and mother have both found manufacturing jobs in a nearby city and have to leave the house early and return late. They find the change to a new city, language, and culture to be "drastic," yet they think their daughter is safe in the school and is acquiring English while keeping up with the school's challenging curriculum. The father approves of the kind of personal identity teachers appear to value for her. He says, "They [the faculty] are vigilant of the well-being of the students so that they always follow the correct paths of life."

THE EMERGENCE OF EXHIBITIONS IN THE SCHOOL'S HISTORY

Exhibitions became a key middle-grades practice during a turbulent period of United City school district reforms. The practice gave teachers and planners an integrative and inventive solution to a daunting challenge: how to bring together a new philosophy of learning, an infusion of technology tools, and a policy shift to including most students with disabilities in heterogeneous classroom learning. The three challenges arose together in the early 1990s when United City was identified by the state department of education as a district that required radical change. All the while that United City was engaged in change, it was developing a new middle school—initially grades 7 and 8 and eventually grades 6 to 8—which became the "laboratory" for inventing new ways to teach United City adolescents and putting new approaches into practice.

These changes were precipitated by the district's dismal failure on state assessments. While United City is a star reform district today, in 1992 it was on the brink of state takeover. Out of 52 areas that the state investigated in a statewide assessment, United City was failing in 40. Student attendance, dropout and transfer rates, and scores on standardized tests were below state averages. The state gave the district a window of 5 years to demonstrate radical improvements. The state department of education ordered the city to develop a corrective action plan (CAP) that would address systematically all 40 problem areas. When the state required that United City put new leadership in place, the district found a new superintendent and director of curriculum by looking at the two areas where the district had scored well in the assessment: its gifted and talented program and bilingual programs. These new district leaders saw the assessment debacle as an opportunity to rethink their assumptions, educational programs, and classroom practices.

Curriculum Change

"We went through a paradigm shift in how we thought about the curriculum and learning," says Frank Barrigg, the former director of bilingual education in United City who was recruited by the state to become the new director of curriculum at the beginning of the reform period. "We changed our thinking from a remedial, deficit perspective—'fixing' Spanish-speaking, low-income kids—to a learning-to-learn perspective and to the view that students are intellectually able," he continues. Teachers for too long had focused on remediating isolated, basic skills rather than on helping students develop advanced literacy and inquiry skills. Students had too few opportunities to understand the important concepts and ways of knowing that were becoming the focus of national curriculum reform and national and district standards and assessments. The district assigned a small group of teachers and supervisors to develop a plan to fundamentally improve the quality of education in the district—or surrender local autonomy.

"Our curriculum change was teacher-led, not a top-down revolution, and one we would apply to every individual student," said the curriculum director. This new perspective incorporated cooperative learning approaches that encouraged students to actively construct knowledge with their peers. Through their 5-year CAP, the district worked incrementally to bring these curriculum reforms into the entire district, beginning with grades K–3, then 4–6, then 7–8, and, most recently, the high school. The goal was to produce a curriculum that supported the development of thinking, reasoning, and collaboration skills in all disciplines. This active learning philosophy opened the door to waves of change that included the following:

- Replacing basal readers with authentic literature and a choice of texts
- Stocking classroom libraries and encouraging prolific reading
- Moving from isolated 37–minute periods to block scheduling
- Changing the physical layout of classrooms from fixed rows to worktables
- Placing computers and software tools in each classroom

The shift to cooperative learning meant a radical change in the teacher's role from an expert to a coach who encourages students to take responsibility for their learning. Without two critical decisions by the curriculum planning group, teachers might have been resistant to and overwhelmed by these changes. One was to make changes in stages, beginning with the elementary grades, moving to the middle school, and then the high school.

The other was to make changes voluntary while providing teachers enticing incentives for change. Teachers who chose to change would have refurbished classrooms with libraries, student worktables, and computers and software tools.

The district began assigning a mentor to every new teacher who entered the system. From the opening of the school, Da Vinci students were placed into heterogeneous classrooms where they sat at tables rather than in rows, so they could participate easily in small-group learning.

At the same time, state-level changes in school financing brought new funds to support these curriculum changes. A successful class action lawsuit charging disproportionate funding allowed about 30 urban districts in the state to win increased funding. The passage of the Quality Education Act increased the United City budget from $37.8 million in 1989 to $100 million in 1997. This group of urban school districts became the first cohort of whole-school reform schools when the state subsequently embarked on a statewide reform effort.

Technology Changes

In 1993, Bell Atlantic approached United City administrators with an offer to supply new multimedia resources to urban teachers. The district proposed to Bell Atlantic in 1993–94 a technology-supported project for the entire seventh grade of a new middle school (Da Vinci) they were building to deal with overcrowding in the district's K–8 schools. The opportunity came just in time. The walls of the building that was being renovated to become Da Vinci had just been torn apart to remove asbestos. Bell Atlantic wired every classroom and provided all 135 incoming students in the first Da Vinci seventh grade and the school faculty (20 teachers) with home desktop computers, along with access to the Internet, e-mail, word processing, and database software. In addition, Bell Atlantic provided computers for the school. The district called this groundbreaking venture Project Explore.

"The new Da Vinci Middle School became the testing ground for reforms that would put computers in the hands of low-income children, enabling them to acquire technical and intellectual skills that could provide them a foundation for academic success," explains the curriculum director, Barrigg. With the support of the Center for Children and Technology (CCT) at Education Development Center's New York City office, the Da Vinci faculty then trained the seventh graders and their families in using their new computers.[2]

While subsequent groups of seventh graders did not receive home computers, by 1998 all seventh graders had access to laptops that they could carry between home and school. "Teachers, you'd better get ready! These Laptop Kids—it's 115 kids you can't teach in the old way" (Barrigg). Throughout this period, teachers took on the challenge of deciding how to best use technology as a learning tool. The new curriculum changes called for active, inquiry learning and student cooperation. What would this look like? How could these technology resources best promote challenging intellectual inquiry? And what students should be in the classroom? Is computer-supported, active learning for every child? Could it help students with disabilities learn?

Special Education Changes

"If you focus your experiment on just the honors students or just the gifted or just this group or that group, you have really limited data coming out," says the curriculum director. United City leaders initially did not plan to include students with disabilities in their reforms, but the head of special education insisted. "The director was absolutely tugging at everyone, even as early as 1989–1990, to have a lot more inclusion." The district took its first steps away from a self-contained special education model in 1990 by including two or three students in selected mainstream classes. As technology became available, the philosophy changed from tracking to heterogeneous grouping, and toward a curriculum based on the idea that students with diverse academic and linguistic skills and experience can build knowledge together.

The Project Explore group in 1993 included several students with disabilities. Says the curriculum director:

> The logic behind self-contained [classrooms] disappeared. It became indefensible. There was no reason to exclude these students other than extreme situations. I don't credit any single thing—it wasn't technology, it wasn't inclusion experiments, it wasn't just the curriculum or the structural changes. All of those things happening together created a situation in which it became apparent to people that it [separating students with disabilities] did not make sense.

The district leaders believed that although all students are competent if provided the cognitive tools for learning, most students also face obstacles. Having a disability is an obstacle; other obstacles are the effects of recent immigration status, lack of language proficiency, or poverty. Schools in the district began to look for inclusive practices that would address all or at least many of these challenges. As a district reform leader describes it, parents of students with disabilities were the first ones to say, "Whatever is right for my child is right for the child that is sitting across the table from him. I don't want my child to be placed out of district in another school. I want him or her to stay here, so what can you do to help us make this happen?" The reform leader went on, "That's how we went forward to start to look at a system of *interventions* and not a system of classification."

Exhibitions Integrate the Reforms

Da Vinci became the crucible for inventing *how* to achieve integration in a consistent way in the classrooms across the whole school. Exhibitions emerged as the ideal practice for bringing together changes in curriculum and instruction, the availability of technology tools, and the inclusion of students with disabilities in mainstream learning. Exhibitions fit the cooperative learning model embraced by the district and allowed students to initially focus on oral English skills. Exhibitions benefited from student access to the Internet, which exploded into American school learning environments during the Bell Atlantic "experiment" in United City. And exhibitions pushed low-income Latino students into the mainstream with informational and technology tools. Kathleen Tully, Bell Atlantic's project manager of Project Explore, explains:

> The real value here is the students are encouraged to evaluate the information and make decisions regarding the importance and relevance of the data. No longer do they have one textbook that tells them all they need to know about a topic. They do collaborative research and, as a class, determine the facts that are important for them to know and remember.

While educators from Da Vinci first heard the term *exhibition* at early exploratory meetings with the Coalition of Essential Schools, they designed their own version to reflect their core beliefs and necessary changes in the districts' educational policies. Technology could support students in the kinds of research, writing, and presenting that exhibitions require. Consistent with the school's belief in a family-oriented learning environment, families took many active roles in exhibitions. Consistent with changes in special education policy, students like Karin were expected to participate in exhibitions and received varied forms of support to succeed. Exhibitions put into practice the idea that when students teach others, they are better able to make the transition from Spanish to English. Out of a district-level crisis and surge of reform, the school fashioned a classroom practice that put district goals into practice in everyday school learning.

Throughout this early period, Da Vinci teachers and its small number of administrators (a principal and a facilitator) made exhibitions come together. The bilingual director describes this period of innovation in the school as a time of "squabbles, a lot of crying, a lot of tears, a lot of bloodshed, *as in any family*." Teachers disagreed about how to organize the school around exhibitions and use equipment most effectively. They discussed how to engage parents, and how students in the bilingual program could do exhibitions in Spanish. What helped them, the pioneer teachers think, was the strong role that the district and school leaders gave them in making early decisions. One of those teachers remembers it this way:

> We were always asked and always spoke our minds. We didn't
> agree on everything. . . . When people feel important, they rise
> to the occasion. Teachers, students, and parents had ownership
> in the school and what you get back in return is highly moti-
> vated teachers who encourage highly motivated students.
> That's why I think the beginning was very successful. Our job
> was to take the curriculum guidelines for United City and use
> our own uniqueness in how we designed learning approaches
> that make use of technology tools.

Nevertheless, making exhibitions the core of learning would require problem solving and invention from the whole school. Many students were new to the school and to American culture, many acquiring English as a second language, most facing risks associated with poverty, and many also coping with learning disabilities or cognitive delay. Teachers faced daunting challenges in designing a school that could make inquiry, research, and technology-based presentations the core of learning.

In embedding exhibitions in Da Vinci in the mid-1990s teachers also faced additional practical problems, such as how to respond to individual students' needs in chronically overcrowded classrooms. And how should they assess this kind of learning? For example, how important is it for students to use correct spelling and grammar on exhibition slides and posters? How should students without any English participate? How can exhibitions offer sufficient support for struggling learners and adequate intellectual challenge for academically advanced students? Given how much responsibility students have for working together and learning from one another, how can the school help them manage conflicts that may disrupt cooperative work?

MAKING EXHIBITIONS WORK FOR ALL

Da Vinci developed several kinds of academic and social support that brought students with highly diverse academic abilities into a cooperative learning environment. The school designed an exhibition approach—introduced at the beginning of this chapter—that includes six kinds of academic and social support.

1. All students have access to technology tools that support exhibitions.
2. Adults provide instructional scaffolding to meet individual student needs.
3. Students are expected to assist one another with exhibitions.
4. Transitioning second-language learners get assistance with exhibitions.
5. Students receive social and emotional support for collaborative learning.
6. Teachers work together to assess and improve exhibitions.

Access to Technology Tools

All the various uses of technology in the school—both "low tech," such as overhead projectors, and "high tech" uses of the Internet and presentation software—are designed to assist students in learning and in communicating what they learn to others. Figure 3.4 lists the various ways that technology tools directly assist Da Vinci students in each of the major phases of exhibition learning: gathering information, connecting and organizing information, and presenting findings. Two additional phases, managing exhibitions and assessing learning, provide direct support to teachers. Teaching and management challenges arise as teachers need to keep track of many students' presentations and plan complex public events where many students show their work. Storing and assessing students' exhibitions require teachers to be able to retrieve students' presentations. Electronic portfolios are used to collect and store students work over 3 years. These sources of support are "transparent" in that they are basic to what makes exhibitions work, yet have become so much a way of life in the school that they don't stand out. As one teacher puts it, "Technology is just a source of help, it's in the background. The important thing . . . what we work toward, is students' learning to learn and share what they know."

Figure 3.4. Transparent Technology Support for Learning through Exhibitions

Technology applications	Support for learning
	Students gather information
Internet	• Search relevant information • Find/retrieve relevant photos, primary source documents (diaries, journals, chronicles)
CD-ROM	• Gather information (encyclopedia, specialized databases) • Retrieve visual information, video clips • Domain-specific documents, photographs, texts • On-line encyclopedia
	Students connect and organize information
Filing and word processing	• Take notes on main ideas in reading and interviews • Store and organize information • Compose, revise, and edit text
	Students present findings
Word processing/ spelling and grammar check	• Edit for Standard English • Self-assess spelling, mechanical errors
PowerPoint	• Organize information by category • Prioritize information, identify key facts • Summarize key information concisely • Sequence ideas and information
Multimedia tools	• Scan in photos, documents, posters • Illustrate ideas and information with visuals • Integrate sound, video clips, animation • Organize presentation
	Teachers manage exhibitions
Calendars Time lines Databases	• Develop production schedule for events • Store students' grades and assessments • Store parents' addresses • Develop lesson plans
	Teachers assess completed projects
Electronic portfolio	• Store individual student exhibitions and individual assignments • Store group exhibitions (zip discs)

Learning the tools. While technology provides many kinds of support, it also can be daunting to a new user. Incoming sixth graders get acculturated to the technology tools for exhibitions early on. The following is an example of a scene that took place in a sixth-grade classroom:

> "Choose a state, *any state* in the country, from this U.S. map. That's *your* state." In the computer lab, pairs of sixth-grade students, including Karin and a partner, sit at computers, looking up at a map of the United States projected from the teacher's computer against the entire back wall of the room. In pairs, students will create a "mini-exhibition," using several websites to find out everything they can about the state.

These students will gather information about the climate, economy, number of big cities, and other special information about "their state," using an Internet address the teacher provides. When Karin was in this class, she and her partner chose Montana, a state they had seen in a movie about rodeos. The students will develop a show that is four slides long to present what they have learned to the rest of the class.

Actually, socialization into presentations began for Karin in September in sixth grade, when she was assigned in her English class to write a paragraph about a family member and read it aloud to one other student, as a way to learn to listen to and critique each other's work. This computer lab activity builds on that classroom experience by adding technology tools for research and presentation, while broadening students' knowledge of U.S. geography. The computer teacher, Janis Rojas, explains that inducting students into this way of learning is a step-by-step process.

> It starts very small. They work in groups, then in front of the whole class, and by the time they are in the seventh grade they are presenting to other classes. With the support they get—and there is a lot in this school—they are confident to do it because they have done it over and over again. They are elected to take an active role and they step up to the plate.

Opportunities for advanced users. These "training" experiences level the playing field for entering students, so that all have equal opportunity and the support they need to be comfortable with groupwork, voicing their ideas, and using computer tools. And some students want more than this basic training. "I can do fifty trillion things on the computer." David looks older than a seventh grader in his Harry Potter glasses, eyebrows askew over intense eyes. Whether or not a class assignment requires computer tools, he scans most of his assignments into his on-line portfolio. And he begs his computer teacher to throw technical challenges his way.

> I scan things. When the President came here [Clinton visited United City briefly in 1998 because of the technology integration], we did a video conference and recorded it and we animated it. Mr. Martinez did that, I just helped. I've built seven web pages, some for other people. I do HTML or Page Builder.

David displays his recent mathematics exhibition in PowerPoint, a summary of what he's learned in mathematics over the past 3 months. Although he is clearly proud of that display, he is most excited to describe how his computer skills have blossomed. Throughout the year, the computer teacher has allowed David to become his apprentice, helping on special projects. David has used publishing software to organize "five homerooms for the yearbook so far. I've taken 300 pictures with my digital camera and downloaded them. About four zip discs." He thinks PowerPoint "shows you what you're doing, and makes it look more professional." He is well aware of the cutting-edge applications that the computer specialists are bringing into the school, the resistance of some faculty, and the endless problems associated with getting new software working. "Like we're trying to get this thing up called Virtual Field trip. They can sit here and go through the Museum of Natural History [in New York City] but it's not working. Glitches." The main challenge for students like David is getting the computer teacher's time to tutor him.

Adult Scaffolding

The school day is organized so that students can get help from adults in class, in resource rooms, and through tutorial before and after school. Karin avails herself of all of these options. Her biggest problem with her part of the 1950s exhibition was the PowerPoint technology. With her teacher's assistance, Karin was able to locate information, organize her findings, and edit her written English. Her investigation also drew on classwork, books and articles, Internet sites, interviews with her mother, and listening to her mother's old phonograph records. She downloaded posters and information from several Internet sites and integrated them into her presentation. But she could not find her way through the procedures for making, revising, sorting, and viewing slides.

During class time, her social studies teacher coached her and her two partners in assembling a 22-step procedure for making a PowerPoint slide.

For example, "(1) slide layout, pick the first box, (2) select the first box for the title, (3) go to Word Art (select), (4) click on word text box, and more. They used the list throughout their preparation and shared it with other students. The students' list of steps was detailed, to help them learn the process, because Karin and some other students cannot recall these procedures even after long use of PowerPoint.

Special education teachers provide direct assistance to students in a resource room and in the classroom. Describing how she helped Karin, the seventh-grade resource room teacher said, "Where I come in is on the ground floor of even just finding out what the research requires and helping her write her piece and get it down into the things they want to use." The teacher made an effort to work in Karin's classroom so that she could help her work well with Tomás and Javier. Separately, in the resource room, she helped Karin identify the key pieces that she needed to develop—a level of individual help that would have taxed the classroom teacher in a class of more than 25 students.

The special education teacher sees herself as part of a team effort to help "get the best out of the kid" and looks to teachers for help with identifying students who are capable of doing more. She says she's been in other schools where the self-fulfilling prophecy about students with disabilities takes over, which she describes as a "hey, they're in special ed and maybe they can't do it type of thing."

> Here [at Da Vinci] it's, "Let's see what he can do, and let's push him to that if he can." And nine out of ten times, kids do succeed to a higher level. We can send these kids to college. They don't have to barely get through high school. I'd like to see that happen, that our kids don't quit school, which often happens, or just barely finish or go to a vocational program, but explore the possibilities of going on to college.

Teachers continually work at coordinating the students' movement between the resource room and classroom so that students don't miss critical material and exacerbate their academic difficulties.

Karin also got early morning help in the school's before-school, extended-day program. "You never know what they are going to need—or *when*," says the special education teacher, who is also one of the extended-day tutors. She describes the approach of the program as "open door" assistance. Karin came particularly for help with organizing information she had found from several different sources and editing her slides for the PowerPoint presentation. Because Karin is "such a proactive kid" in getting assistance, she gets just the help she needs at the right time.

Informal Peer Assistance

Because classes are crowded at Da Vinci, and students can require a good deal of help, informal peer assistance between students is a critical form of support for exhibition learning. As the district envisioned, students mainly sit at tables, and the low buzz is usually from talk about an assignment. In preparing her 1950s exhibition, Karin used a lot of peer help from students in her exhibition group. Javier helped her organize the material for her slides; Tomás gave her feedback on spelling and helped her make short sentences to fit PowerPoint slides. Havier also helped Tomás occasionally with word choice, since his English is less advanced.

Despite her disabilities, Karin is aware when she needs help and uses the system of adult and peer help to get it. The challenge of a peer assistance system for students with disabilities is that they may have difficulty with the self-monitoring that students need in order to ask for help, and their disability may impede their using the help. Marco, a boy with moderate disabilities, and Steven, a boy with more severe learning difficulties, provide two different examples of the limitations of peer support for students with disabilities.

Marco can achieve moderately well but does not always recognize that he needs help. As a result, it's up to others to initiate help for him, and he doesn't always welcome it. In a class studying hurricanes, for example, Marco is paired with another student to use software that actively tracks the development and velocity of active hurricanes. The teacher has projected a swirling mass of red, a real-time image of a hurricane location and velocity, on the back wall of the computer lab from her computer, and students are hurrying to get to the same Internet address with their hurricane software. Marco frowns, moves the cursor, and bangs the mouse, opening the wrong URL. Although his partner pauses three times to point to the right address, Marco perseveres in the wrong address. He gets back on track and involved in the activity only after an observer directly helps him move his cursor to the right spot.

Research literature on students with mild to moderate disabilities finds that students with disabilities may be less likely than typically achieving students to request help and to take an active role in discussion. A student like Marco depends on other students or adults to see his struggle and initiate assistance. This proactive assistance is less likely to be forthcoming if other students are under time pressure to complete their own work and if the activity is not designed to require or at least encourage collaboration.

Some teachers think that the lower functioning special education students are the least likely to benefit from informal peer assistance norms. An observer in a replacement math class working on computation problems writes, "Steven is lost. He stares at the paper and makes a few marks. Other students at his table get up to get help. He stares at his paper, then turns around and talks to boys behind them. They respond but when they are unable to help him, they get back to their work. Steven looks out into space." The Da Vinci staff agonizes about students like Steven. They want to avoid recommending students like him for substantially separate special education classes in the high school, where they feel certain the students will have less stimulating learning and peers. Yet, Steven consistently is lost in a general classroom, even when norms of peer helping are clearly established.

Support for Transitioning Spanish Speakers

Da Vinci's bilingual program is designed to enable students to participate fully in the school's curriculum in their own language while they are acquiring English. Consistent with what some call culturally responsive literacy instruction, the students use their strengths in their home languages to become proficient in reading, speaking, and writing English (Callins, 2004). Da Vinci students get academic support for developing exhibitions in Spanish in their bilingual classes. When they migrate to mainstream classes, the school's informal peer support system works well for them.

Exhibitions in Spanish. Monica, whose father is quoted earlier, enrolled in seventh grade at Da Vinci Middle School 2 weeks after her family emigrated from Colombia. She spoke no English and knew nothing about U.S. or European history. At the end of that year, she and two classmates, Brenda and Patricia—both immigrants from Honduras—stand before their classmates and teachers, guiding them through a PowerPoint presentation about the Holocaust. Their presentation is the culmination of intensive classroom instruction and discussion about World War II and the roots of racism, and weeks of independent research, groupwork, and writing.

Students who come to Da Vinci with little or no English spend up to a year or more in the school's bilingual program, where they learn rigorous content in their first language and concurrently study English as a second language. Monica and her two classmates are engaged in studying the Holocaust in order to acquire the subject-matter knowledge and the ways of learning that are prized at Da Vinci. The idea is that when the girls transition into the mainstream classroom, they will be as expert as other students in developing a topic, researching information, and using technology support.

The exhibitions in the bilingual program are every bit as serious as those in mainstream classes. Along with their oral presentation, each girl has prepared her own written report. Janice's report—85 pages in Spanish—is longer than any of the written reports by English-speaking students in the school that year. "This wasn't just an exercise in reading textbooks and memorizing dates and battles," Janice explains. Exhibitions in Spanish also are meant to build world knowledge and a deep interest in other groups and cultures. Classmates and teachers listen attentively as the girls use a world map to trace Jewish emigration from Germany between 1933 and 1942, describe the destruction of Jewish businesses on "Kristallnacht," and chart the numbers of victims by country.

The girls conclude their presentation with a collection of photos of concentration camps and the liberation of prisoners. Their final words read: *"El Holocausto es y sera una march en nuestras vidas"* [The Holocaust has made a mark on our lives]. Janice was profoundly affected by what she learned and very proud of their "deep investigation." "It made me cry when I saw the photos. I couldn't believe that someone from the same race could do that."

Learning the technical skills of PowerPoint was not the biggest challenge for Monica and her group, since all three girls were familiar with the Internet and the basics of computer use. The biggest obstacle was the lack of Spanish-language information on the Web. This shocked Monica: "All the information should have been in Spanish because the Holocaust is something universal that everyone should know! But like almost all of the Web, everything is in English." Their bilingual program teachers encouraged them to take on the topic anyway and to keep working in Spanish. Brenda, whose English is most advanced, proudly took the job of translating articles from English to Spanish. "We did it all ourselves," she says, "sometimes word by word, with dictionaries."

Transitioning into the regular classroom. When Spanish-speaking students like Monica move into the mainstream classroom, they will have the same exhibition skills as the other students, but they still may not have the full English proficiency they need. Informal peer assistance is one key to their survival and success in engaging in exhibition-focused learning in the regular classroom. A snapshot of two other second-language learners who have transitioned into the regular classroom shows how this informal coaching can help.

"Como se dice?" [How do you say this?] Lisa asks her friend, Cecilia, for English words in her eighth-grade communications class. Lisa, who has just transitioned from the bilingual classroom where she spent the year learning content in Spanish while learning English in ESOL classes, is sitting with Rafael, who also is transitioning from the bilingual program, and Cecilia, who is fluent in Spanish and English. The teacher has assigned an essay on a topic Da Vinci eighth graders talk about a lot: *If you were gradu-*

ating from eighth grade and were offered a very good job, would you take it or go to high school? Why? Cecilia points to a phrase Lisa has written in Spanish on her English paper. She pulls Lisa's paper closer and writes an English translation of Lisa's phrase: "Because later you have a reward." The teacher nods as she walks by, observing this exchange. Later, when the teacher directs the group to exchange papers and edit one another's work, Lisa first exchanges with Cecilia, who asks her to clarify part of the essay: "What do you mean here? You mean your family had to work early in the day because . . . ?" Lisa then turns to edit Rafael's paper, seeing him struggling with the essay.

These interactions point up some conditions—typical of the school—that help to make peer assistance an important source of support for transitioning bilingual students.

- Students are free to draw on either language. The group includes enough members who are strong in different language skills to ensure that there is someone to help everyone.
- Students are at ease with asking for help because they know one another and because such requests are expected.

Further, the teacher deepens the helping structure at a critical point by shifting students from ad hoc helping to structured peer editing, where every student gets feedback from at least one other group member. Finally, students like Lisa bring personal skills to these learning opportunities. She is an ideal partner because she freely asks for help, knowing the school considers that a strength.

Collaborative Planning and Assessment

Exhibitions give students an opportunity to control parts of their learning and to express their ideas in their own language. As a result, exhibitions reveal students' grasp of Standard English and the depth of their reading and understanding. Following a schoolwide Expo with many student presentations, teachers hold a faculty meeting to assess what they have seen. Many teachers are disappointed with the quality of the exhibitions students presented to the entire faculty and more than 100 parents. "I saw too many spelling errors." "It wasn't just the spelling—the exhibitions were all over the place. Some were great, others weak. . . . I won't say *which*. What are we doing?" "This isn't good enough!" "We don't have an assessment of Expo. We just go through it." "How would we assess it?" "Well, why don't we figure this out?" Voices are loud and angry-sounding to an outsider used to more formal, less combative faculty meetings.

This meeting focuses entirely on the criteria for an acceptable exhibition and how to help students meet those criteria. Previously, teachers assigned grades individually for students' exhibitions, but without any common criteria for what constitutes "good work." Over the next hour, the teachers discuss and argue about the goals of schoolwide exhibitions and what to look for in students' presentations. In the week following the Expo, the teachers meet again and agree that they omitted one criterion that was a glaring issue in the exhibitions: the quality of students' writing. They agree that they will all review students' work and help them with editing their English for the next schoolwide exhibition and science fair. Over the next year, they redouble their efforts to refine students' written English by pitching in to edit students' work whenever there is a classroom exhibition, an Expo, or a science fair.

Until recently, when the school organized into teams by grade level, the faculty had few formal structures other than faculty meetings like these for planning and discussing students' needs. Because the school is small and teachers frequently see one another in the hallways or teachers' room, general and special education teachers are usually aware of their students' needs and progress. In contrast with the vocal faculty meetings, that informal consultation is an important but nearly invisible part of the support system for exhibitions.

Social and Emotional Support for Collaborative Learning

"*Immigrant* has become an insult here. I can't stand it." A bilingual teacher is livid at the most recent incident of students who are themselves "new American" harassing students who come to the community—and the school—midyear from another country. Some speak no English and, while their literacy abilities haven't been sorted out, some probably have learning or reading disabilities. The school has developed two structures, mentoring and peer mediation, to deal with conflict and strengthen students' ability to engage in the kind of high-level cooperation that learning requires at Da Vinci.

Mentoring. To manage the high level of collaboration that exhibitions require, students have to be able to work together. Fighting, especially between students with different Latin countries of origin, is one of the school's biggest obstacles to this. Students tend to pick on the newest students, particularly when they don't speak English. To create a safer school, the faculty decided to set aside an hour early in the day for students to meet in groups of six or seven with a mentor. Every teacher and staff member, including the principal, secretary, and support staff, serves as a mentor.

The goal is for at least one adult to know each student individually and understand the social and emotional issues he or she is struggling with. Teachers wrote a curriculum for the program in the summer to guide early morning meetings.

Peer mediation. "Hi, my name is Raymond and this is my sister, Cynthia. We're here to mediate you guys today." Raymond and his sister, both in grade 8, sit at a square table with two girls who have been feuding. They are scowling at each other, but look at Raymond as he begins. "Do you guys know why you were chosen for mediation?" The two girls nod yes. "Right now we're going to tell you the rules. We're not here to choose sides or anything. We're not here to agree with someone and say, 'You're wrong,' or the other way around. There is no cursing, and you guys can't interrupt. If she is speaking [referring to the other mediator], don't say anything, no matter what." Cynthia adds, "Whatever is said here stays between us. We don't go out and tell anybody else, and both of you don't go out and tell anybody else."

The sixth-grade teacher who coaches the mediators explains that certain conflicts, such as those related to drugs and alcohol, require adult involvement, but that students have become skilled in mediating less serious problems. The results show up in the way students cooperate in preparing and giving exhibitions. Students know they have some choice of partners and are encouraged not to just stick with their own social group. Mediation skills provide a context for academic cooperation and achievement.

Exhibitions require students to put aside feuds. Mentoring and peer mediation programs attempt to provide students the social skills to do that, but they also reach beyond the classroom to carry conflict resolution into students' future school and family lives. "Even in your house, when you have your own family and you have your own kids, you are going to be able to teach your kids, 'Okay, this the way you are supposed to handle situations when you're about to burst,'" the peer mediation coach explains. The "feeder" high school for Da Vinci receives a list of the incoming students who are trained mediators. Sixth-grade students in Da Vinci and another United City school mediated a cross-school conflict, and students from the high school mediated a conflict with students from a New York City high school when a serious fight erupted after a football game.

LEADERSHIP CHALLENGES AND CHANGES

Da Vinci Middle School has experienced numerous disruptions, but at each turn viewed them as an opportunity for improvement. While future challenges are largely unpredictable, school leaders have already grappled with or currently are working on several key issues.

- Sustaining effective leadership beyond the founding stage
- Continuing to meet the needs of students with disabilities
- Expanding the uses of technology in the school

Sustaining School Leadership

"He is a father to the kids. Now they'll have him in high school. That's the good part. The hard part is carrying on his leadership," says a faculty member contemplating the impending departure of Principal Fabio. Not surprisingly, in 1999–2000, 6 years after the school's founding, the principal was asked by the district to take on the role of principal of Everett High School, where most Da Vinci students enroll for ninth grade. At that time, the high schools had become the focus for implementing curriculum reforms across the district. Fabio was a logical choice to bring administrative order to the high school and integrate curriculum reforms pushing up from the elementary and middle grades.

Because he is a charismatic figure, entwined with the school's early history and success, the principal's move has tested the depth of the school's philosophy and practice. If one individual's leadership was holding the school together, his departure could have a dire impact on the school. But although faculty members were deeply affected by the principal's departure, they never seemed to question whether they could sustain the school's success without him.

Several factors appear to have contributed to a successful transition to a new administrative team, which included a new principal, new whole-school reform leader, and coordinator of all support services for students. One was the systemic nature of the school's core beliefs, which reside in exhibitions, in the school's network of support structures, and the Da Vinci faculty's vision of instructional technology as a support for inquiry learning rather than as an end in itself.

Another factor was the involvement of faculty in preparing for the change of leadership. Fabio worked closely with teachers in preparing students for the loss of a father figure. No faculty members left the school because of the principal's departure for the high school—an important indicator of faculty involvement in and comfort with administrative changes. Still another factor was the overwhelming support that administrative staff and faculty gave to the incoming principal, who brought a quieter administrative style together with a deep commitment to the school's approach. The school grieved the loss of a unique leader, yet it did not falter in its continuing mission to meet all students' needs.

As the school continues to evolve, faculty with long-standing places in the school may wish to move into leadership roles in the school, which has a very small "top layer." Will the school continue to be able to provide sufficient intellectual challenge for faculty who are poised for more challenging leadership roles? How critical is the continuing involvement of teachers who helped found the school? Are there newer faculty members who are able to carry on the philosophy to the same degree as those who have worked with the reforms from the beginning? If the school is true to its history, the new leadership team will find new opportunities to respond to both internal and external challenges.

Meeting the Needs of All Students with Disabilities

Overall, students with disabilities have a firm sense of belonging at Da Vinci, and most students are able to benefit from the multilayered, individualized support the school provides. At the same time, some groups of students with disabilities do not fare as well as others. Students with mild disabilities are succeeding in Da Vinci because their disabilities are more manageable and because they are able to take advantage of support from other students and from regular education and special education faculty. Eight or nine students with more severe disabilities are working with a modified curriculum in a small separate classroom. Even with cognitive limitations, these students also have opportunities to engage in project work and to integrate their thinking in oral presentations to their peers.

Students with moderate to severe disabilities, who fall somewhere between these two groups and may number 8 to 10 in any given year, pose the greatest challenge for Da Vinci faculty and administrative leaders. Steven, for example, shows enough strengths to be integrated into the regular classroom, yet he is not succeeding, even with a combination of in-class support, peer assistance, resource room help, and, in some subjects, a modified curriculum. One possible solution is a smaller class size for students like Steven, or more staffing, possibly a collaborative teaching arrangement between a specialist and the content teacher within the classroom. So far, budgetary constraints prohibit this arrangement, and teachers and administrators continue to consider how to provide more support to students such as Steven.

The 1997 reauthorized Individuals with Disabilities Education Act will continue to mandate that the school integrate students with disabilities in the "least restrictive setting"—usually the mainstream classroom. Yet the faculty knows that even with many forms of support, a rigorous, project-oriented classroom is too difficult for some students. The continuing hard question for faculty in this school is how to prepare students with disabilities, many of whom are not proficient in English, for participation in high-stakes statewide testing. And for the many students (more than 100 in 1999) who are not identified with specific disabilities but require accommodations to be successful, how can the limited staff provide all of the help that students need? At the same time, the school's overall success in including students with disabilities in the rigors of project learning and exhibitions in heterogeneous classes offers hopeful images to schools that are newer to inclusive practices.

Expanding Uses of Technology

For several years, exhibitions have allowed students to use many technological tools and resources to build and present their knowledge to one another. A next challenge, according to the computer coordinator for Da Vinci, is to broaden technology support for exhibitions and other kinds of inquiry learning by connecting students with networks of learners in and beyond United City. Students have begun to use, for example, weather tracking software and "virtual" field trip technology. Because some teachers are more ready than others to expand to global problem-solving uses of technology, the challenge for the computer specialist is to work with teachers to stretch beyond the familiar uses that are associated with exhibitions.

Another challenge is to more fully use the resources of computer technology to support students' writing development. The focus on oral exhibitions probably reflects the district's early focus on building oral English skills. But success in high school and beyond requires students to be able to write informational, comparative, expressive/reflective, and persuasive texts and to develop a topic with an extended and detailed argument. Word processing software provides excellent support for revision, but only in a context where extended writing is an integral part of the curriculum.

The equipment from the early infusion of Bell Atlantic support and subsequent funding outlays is now outdated, presenting an additional challenge. If technology is to continue to be a rich, supportive context for exhibitions, keeping up with new and cost-effective technologies will be essential. While replacing equipment will not be a simple matter, the benefits of technology for low-income minority students are so well established in Da Vinci, and so embedded in the vision held by the district as a whole, that technology support for exhibitions, and for learning in general, is likely to remain a high priority for the district.

4

Investigations in Carter-Dean Middle School

So the question once again is, What did you learn about cultures? You all did research on a culture, and you all had a chance to write a paper on what you learned about a culture. So now I want you to do a *cross talk* and tell us what you learned about the culture that you researched. And I pass to Nathan.

Nathan's sixth-grade classmates are sitting in a large circle and turn to focus on Nathan as their teacher, Carolyn Potter, turns the conversation over to her students. For several weeks they have been reading, thinking, and writing about their own cultures and those far beyond their city, St. Ellen. To shed light on the big question, "What is culture?" students have worked in groups of four or five to select a culture in the world, research it, and write about it. They have been reading about the customs, arts, and geography of their culture, and collecting folk tales and other literature of the society they chose. Each group has produced a written report about its findings.

The students themselves represent different cultures and backgrounds. A majority of students in the class are African American and live in the inner city; the other students are White and live in more affluent surrounding communities. Nathan is an eager student who comes to the school from the inner city. Several of the students, including Jonathan and Karen in the following scene, both White students from outlying communities, have disabilities that make learning particularly challenging.

Nathan: Thank you, Mrs. Potter. Culture is sort of, like, it describes the rituals and beliefs, and the way they dress. And . . . [he looks around to see whose hand is up now] I pass to Jonathan.
Jonathan: Thank you, Nathan. I think culture is *beliefs*. The way you act around your family, the things that you eat, and the

> environment you grow up in. And I pass to . . . [turns head,
> seeing Steven's hand up] Steven.
> *Steven:* Thank you, Jonathan. I believe it is everything you do every
> day. Like your daily life. And I pass to Karen [with a broad,
> shy grin].

This formally structured conversation, which students and teachers
in the school call "cross talk," continues until every student who wishes to
speak has spoken. Students always address one another by name when they
pass on the speaking turn, and they thank one another when they receive
the turn. The students focus rapt attention on the individual speaker until
he or she has finished and passed to another student. No one interrupts a
speaker. Red-headed Karen speaks next.

> *Karen:* Thank you, Steven. I think culture is everything—traditions,
> customs, beliefs, how they get their education. And I pass to . . .
> [looks around and sees Kinesha's hand up] Kinesha.
> *Kinesha:* Thank you, Karen. What I learned about my culture is that
> Africans like music, and they like to do a lot of dancing, and
> they wear special clothing like Kente cloth.

This particular cross talk is the culmination of a 10-week investigation of what culture means and how cultures differ in a unit titled "Myths,
Legends, and Folk Tales" that all sixth graders are doing in all of the core
subjects. At the beginning of this unit, Potter engaged the class in an "anchor experience" to immerse them in the idea of culture. They viewed an
ethnographic film of seal hunting in far northern Canada. A Netsilik father and son take turns bending over a seal blow hole for 8 hours until they
finally thrust a harpoon through the hole and kill the seal. They gather in
an ice house with other families to cut it apart and share it. Students talked
about how surprising it is to see raw meat divided this way and debated
why the family did not keep the seal all for itself. They cross talked about
how the situation is similar to or different from ones they experience in
their own families.

As the next phase of the unit, students generated a long list of questions about families and cultures. They divided into small working groups
("pods") where they each chose a world culture and used books, articles,
and the Internet to probe into the questions they had generated. They took
trips to the nearby science museum to look at exhibits of different groups.
Each group selected one of the folk tales they had collected and drama-
tized it for the rest of the class and then cross talked about what messages
come across in the tales. Each pod designed a game that uses important

information about that culture, as well as mathematics concepts. They used an on-line Knowledge Forum to post and respond to the big questions they came up with about culture, continuing the cross talk about culture on their computers. Each pod used word processing software to write a folk tale with a similar structure to ones they had read. Their own folk tales became a part of a book. The folk tale and pod report are considered "consequential tasks"—that is, final products in which students pull together their new knowledge and share it with others.

In Carter-Dean Middle School, investigations are a pervasive, school-wide practice—the school's signature practice. They take place across an entire grade level and may take up to 12 weeks. All involve four core subjects of social studies, science, mathematics, and literature, and some also involve music, art, industrial technology, family and consumer science, and/or physical education. Although forms of investigation take place in many schools, usually within particular subject areas as final projects, the particular structure of investigations outlined in Figure 4.1 is unique to Carter-Dean.

The context of every investigation is a full, interdisciplinary curriculum unit that teachers develop themselves with the assistance of curriculum and content experts. Cooperative structures such as cross talk encourage each student to talk and to learn from other students. Technology is a presence in every stage of an investigation. While literacy is the province of language arts in most schools, at Carter-Dean all teachers are responsible for teaching

Figure 4.1. Investigations at Carter-Dean

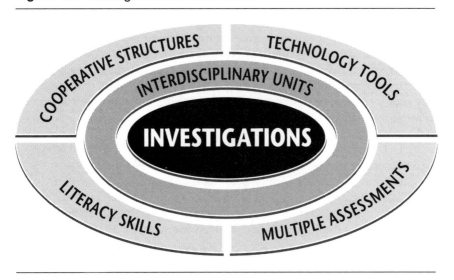

the reading, writing, and discussion skills that students need in order to engage in scholarly learning. Students are responsible for and assessed on the basis of both their cooperative and individual work. All Carter-Dean investigations share a structure that the school assembled with careful consideration of research on learning and their students' particular strengths and needs as adolescent learners (Morocco, Clark-Chiarelli, & Aguilar, 2002).

In investigations, students focus their content learning on one big topic and a few overarching questions of social and scientific importance. Over about 12 weeks, students in an entire grade level study the topic and share their learning. The main features of Carter-Dean investigations, which are portrayed in Figure 4.1, include the following:

- *Interdisciplinary curriculum units* provide a predictable structure for investigations.
- *Cooperative learning structures* build student voice and facilitate adult support.
- *Technology tools* scaffold inquiry and writing.
- *Literacy skills* for investigations are taught by all faculty members.
- *Classroom assessment* systems reward cooperative investigation.

Students take on compelling questions that to an observer seem daunting for 11- or 12-year-olds: What makes a city work? How have people survived in the Alaskan environment? What are our responsibilities to our planet, and how are we accountable? They identify smaller, often controversial issues to study within those larger questions: Should products be tested on plants and animals? Who should pay for cleaning up pollution? What can be done about global warming? Cross talk and other kinds of peer talk thread through these investigations, bringing students back again and again in every phase of the investigation to share and connect ideas or solve problems in how they are doing their work. They may engage in cross talk to understand a reading, debrief a test, or even marshal arguments in favor of what one student describes as "ditching one required reading for a more interesting one."

MEET A SCHOOL FOR THOUGHT

Carter-Dean Middle School is a medium-sized school of approximately 500 students situated off a busy four-lane road that cuts through the city of St. Ellen. The hyphenated name reflects the school's dual commitments to learning and to service to society. One namesake was a physicist and a Nobel laureate whose studies of x-rays led to his discovery of changes in wavelength of high-energy electromagnetic radiation. The other was an African American surgeon and pioneer in developing techniques for processing and storing blood plasma for use in transfusion. He helped establish blood banks during World War II and became the first director of the American Red Cross Blood Bank. The school's mission statement emphasizes the traditions of both scholarship and social responsibility from its namesakes:

> Carter-Dean fosters a community of learners which develops leadership skills in our students to live in a democratic society.

Carter-Dean is a magnet school that identifies itself as a "Schools for Thought," a designation based on the work of James McDonnell, who wrote a book with that title and has funded a number of major cognitive scientists whose work the school drew on in its founding.

Opened in September 1996, the school is light and welcoming. The main office, gym, and cafeteria open off a large foyer with an atrium ceiling. One sign that science is important in the school is the presence of the Science Theater, just beyond the foyer. It has satellite hookups, facilities for videotaping student projects, and ample space for developing math and science forums. The classrooms are located in a tower wide enough to house a grade level on each floor, which facilitates students' collaborative work on interdisciplinary units within grade levels. On the third floor, where the eighth graders are housed, bulletin boards are loaded with student papers; the principal jokes that the fire department said that the amount of writing they do is causing a fire hazard. Large glass windows on the inside wall allow students to peer down into the big library below, an important learning and media center for the school.

By design, Carter-Dean is adjacent to the St. Ellen Science Center. This and other museums in the city—the Botanical Gardens, St. Ellen Zoo, and St. Ellen Art Museum—extend students' learning beyond the school and are represented on the school's advisory board. Signs of the school and museum partnership are visible. The cafeteria, called Galaxy Too, is named after the Science Museum's café, Galaxy. A huge mound of flexible grey vinyl, big as a collapsed elephant, lies in one part of a first-floor classroom—the result of a school and Science Center collaboration. It's an inflatable dome that students designed and constructed out of plastic and vinyl. The project began when seventh graders started their study of triangles and became interested in the structure of a geodesic dome. Rather than borrow one from the next-door museum, they used a Science Center dome as a model to construct one of their own. They used it as a "star dome" with hanging models of constellations. In a reversal of the usual, the

Science Center asked the school to lend the dome to the museum for its exhibits.

Tools and products of investigations are all around the school. Out in the second-floor hallway, visible to anyone on that floor, is a consequential task from a unit on cities. Students constructed a replica of a city on an 18-inch-high platform with commercial and residential buildings, a power station, a park, and structures to show sewer and electrical lines. Most classrooms have nine computers lined along one wall that are networked with one another and the Web. Bulletin boards and blackboards cover another wall, along with a classroom library. A media center holds another 20 computers and organizes collections of materials by topic.

Students

By most standards, Carter-Dean is a medium-sized middle school, with a student population of 515 students. Students are selected by lottery, the procedure used for all magnet schools in the city. The racial composition has been stipulated by court desegregation orders for magnet schools and, as of 1999, must be 60% Black and 40% White, with a deviation of 5% allowed. Over one third (37%) of the student body is Caucasian; students who identify themselves as African American constitute 61%, and a small percentage, 2%, fall within the categories of Asian, Latino/Hispanic, and Native American. Approximately 65% of the students are in free or reduced-price lunch programs. No students have limited English proficiency.

Between 1999 and 2002, the percentage of students with identified disabilities ranged from 12 to 17.5%. These students also are selected by lottery. Because the school has a strong reputation for high levels of support and achievement for students with disabilities, a steady stream of families with children with disabilities applies to the new sixth grade each year. Except for a class of 10 students with more severe disabilities, whose parents strongly advocated for a separate classroom, students with disabilities are included in the regular classrooms, all of which are heterogeneously grouped. As a parent of a child with disabilities in the first graduating class says, "Gifted and special, all are grouped together. No one is left out. Everyone has something to contribute."

Coming into the school for the first time is a shock for most sixth graders, whichever community they come from. Toward the end of his first year in the school, a sixth-grade boy from inner-city St. Ellen talks about how different the school is from "regular schools." "It's school because you learn things, but it's learning in a different way. In my old school, you just sat in your seat and raised your hand for everything. In Carter-Dean you don't really raise your hand; you ask the kids around you." However, the expectation that all students talk about their learning has been hard for him. "Here you talk all the time. I'm really not that kind of person who likes to talk in the cross talk or anything. At the beginning of the year I really didn't talk at all; I just sat in my seat." He thinks he has changed some: "Now I ask questions because I want to learn something and not just sit there." When asked directly what the school is like, students from across the grade levels use words such as "scientific," "research," "hard learning," "thinking," "investigate," "anchor," "cross talk," "Knowledge Forum," "pods," "reciprocal teaching," and "culminating tasks."

The Faculty

A substantial number of faculty members were a part of the founding of the school in the early to mid-1990s and stayed in the school throughout the decade. When new faculty members come, they are assigned a mentor to help them learn the particular forms of teaching and learning that are signatures of this school. The faculty is ethnically diverse. Over half are African American, including the four members of the administrative team: principal, administrative principal, instructional coordinator, and program coordinator. Alvera Williams, the principal, was one of the first African American women to attend an all-White high school in the city. Bringing together students with different cultural and economic backgrounds in a common goal "to understand and care about the world" is Williams's mission. The Carter-Dean teaching staff includes 25 content-area teachers, 6 special education teachers, and 8 teacher assistants. The Science Center provides the school with a full-time science specialist who assists with curriculum design for all disciplines and serves as a liaison to the Science Center.

The very first cohort of teachers was trained in the school's investigative model in 1996, the summer before the school opened. Some students participated in that summer institute so that teachers could practice using an investigative cycle directly with students. The tradition of a summer school with incoming sixth-grade students has continued, and it is a time for veteran teachers to keep honing their practices and for new teachers to learn the schools for thought approach. In 1999, the principal felt that teachers could be learning more from one another on a day-to-day basis throughout the year, so she arranged for a group from a local university to come in and train teachers in peer coaching (Nave, 2000; Showers & Joyce, 1996).

Performance on Standardized Tests

The school has performed strongly among St. Ellen magnet schools from the beginning of statewide testing and continues to do so in almost all areas. Essentially, sixth-grade students enter the school with the same content and reading scores as sixth graders in the other magnet schools. However, by eighth grade, students in this school outperform the other magnet school students in the major content areas. Even in mathematics, where the school has had challenging targets to reach—10% improvement or more each year—the school is a top performer among the magnet schools and across the district.

More specifically, in 2000 in communication arts, 69% of Carter-Dean seventh graders scored at the nearing proficiency, proficient, or advanced proficient levels, in contrast with an average of 51% of students in other magnet schools. In science that same year, eighth graders without disabilities scored at the 57th percentile as compared with the 24th percentile on average in other magnet schools. Students with disabilities show similar trends. Thirty-one percent of seventh-grade students with disabilities scored at the nearing proficiency, proficient, or advanced proficient levels in communication arts as compared with an average of 19% in other magnet schools in 2000. Twenty-four percent of students with disabilities performed at the lowest level ("Step 1") compared with 55% of students with disabilities at other magnet schools. In social studies in 2000, 50% of Carter-Dean eighth-grade students with disabilities scored at the advanced proficient level, compared with an average of 4% of students with disabilities at other magnet schools.

The school's mathematics achievement has always been above the 50th percentile, and in 2002, the school's rankings were at the 60th percentile. Social studies and communication arts also exhibited dramatic gains in 2002. In 2003, the school ranked first among the district's seven magnet middle schools (excluding the gifted and talented middle school) in mathematics, and second in language and in reading. In 2004, Carter-Dean ranked second in mathematics and communication arts and third in reading. Yet, the "wolf is always at the door." The tension between providing students the freedom to explore in investigations and ensuring that they know the kinds of information required on statewide tests is always present.

CORE BELIEFS BEHIND INVESTIGATIONS

Behind the pervasive use of investigations across all grade levels, subject areas, and classrooms in Carter-Dean, lie some consistent ideas about learning, adolescents, and society. These ideas are evident in every conversation in classrooms and hallways; in the designs for learning in the curriculum units that teachers write together as grade-level teams; in the school's mission statement; and in the ways that students, teachers, and community members talk about the school. Together these beliefs define what Carter-Dean means by a School for Thought. They have inspired and guided the school since it was designed, with the help of cognitive scientists, in the early to mid-1990s. Three beliefs about learning stand out.

- *Students as scholars.* With teacher support and scaffolding, young adolescents are capable of carrying out scholarly investigations into the critical questions that face our society.
- *Collaborative learning communities.* Important understandings develop through intimate partnerships and structured joint explorations with experts in and beyond the school.
- *Social equity and responsibility.* All students have ideas to share and contributions to make to their school and society.

Students as Scholars

Carter-Dean adults believe the purpose of education is for individuals to understand the true dilemmas of human society. In her always formal and dignified way of speaking, the principal, Alvera Williams, is adamant about the idea.

At Carter-Dean we *refuse* to believe that the connection between poverty and academic failure is a cycle that cannot be broken. We believe that students will achieve up to a school's expectations, and we have continued to verbalize, require, and demonstrate examples of our expectations.

Faculty members think that building a society that respects and supports people of different cultures and economic levels is a complex challenge that does not necessarily lend itself to simple solutions. They think these dilemmas have to be examined from several perspectives, through the lenses of science, anthropology, geography, fables and myths, and mathematics. They believe that all students are capable of building knowledge about real-world issues and that each student has experiences and some expertise to bring to learning. In engaging students in these big questions, the adults expect students to build several kinds of understandings, including understanding important facts and information, ways to investigate a question or problem, and the *purposes* of a social/scientific investigation. Students are expected to take charge of acquiring their own investigative skills.

These beliefs and understanding goals are consistent with learning theories that see humans as intellectually generative and active participants in building knowledge (Bransford, Brown, & Cocking, 2000). In order to become good investigators, students have to practice with the real thing. They need to participate in "authentic tasks" that focus on big questions of relevance beyond school, require them to engage in higher level thinking, and focus on concepts, information, and ideas that experts in the field deem important (Newmann & Associates, 1996). Also, students are likely to be able to apply tools of investigation—posing questions, gathering information, reading graphs and charts, interviewing experts—to new questions if they learn to use the tools in situations and around questions that arouse their curiosity and desire to learn (Guthrie & Alvermann, 1999).

Carter-Dean teachers believe that teachers have a critical role to play in investigative learning, not as the "sage on the stage" but as the "guide on the side." The Carter-Dean brochure says that "students and teachers are co-learners, rather than the traditional view of teachers as disseminators of knowledge and students as empty vessels to fill." In *The Dreamkeepers* (1994), her study of culturally relevant teaching, Ladson-Billings argues that teachers of African American children are "culturally responsive" when they take the role of guide or coach to help students work toward excellence and connect their learning to a wider community. Yet, this guide also can directly teach students the content information and learning skills they need in order to work on the big questions.

Some cognitive scientists consider this integration of discovery and direct instruction to be at the heart of inquiry learning (Brown & Campione, 1994, 1996). Students' investigation of world cultures described in the opening vignette of this chapter combines exploration and skill development, very like the idea of "guided discovery" that Ann Brown and colleagues (Brown & Campione, 1994) characterized as a middle ground between didactic teaching and discovery learning. Carter-Dean teachers believe that skills—such as using reference books, cross talk, and essay writing—have to be made explicit and directly taught to students. They believe that students from lower income families with less formal schooling in particular need to have the directions and procedures that are required by the school culture made explicit through direct instruction as well as discovery activities (Delpit, 1995).

Communities of Learners

Carter-Dean teachers believe that interactions with others in and beyond the school play an essential role in building knowledge (Bransford, Brown, & Cocking, 2000; Palincsar & Rupert-Herrenkohl, 1999). The idea that people build understanding through talking with one another is visible in cross talk and in the pod structure, which requires members to answer one another's questions before they bring a question to the teacher and where students are evaluated for their group products as well as their individual contributions. Because all students at one grade level investigate the same overarching question, the grade level is an important unit of cooperation and conversation in the school. Teacher planning at each grade level focuses extensively on designing ways that students can serve as intellectual partners to one another within a unit. Clubs, which almost all teachers in the school help to facilitate, provide additional ways for students to share and build ideas together. And the Carter-Dean learning community extends beyond the school to the museums that are represented on the school's advisory board and serve as sites for information gathering beyond the school. Ten colleges and universities also partner with the school to place interns, provide professional development, and help design curriculum units.

Social Equity and Responsibility

Teachers design what Asa Hilliard (2002) calls a "pluralistic curriculum"—one that "paints an accurate picture of the total human experience, no matter what events we choose to examine" (p. 99). Hilliard argues that a truthful portrayal of human events will instantly force a pluralization of the curriculum. A pluralistic curriculum includes all students in investigating real events and real truths about the world and human experience. Curriculum units bring in what teachers consider the "hard information"— the truth about human problems, consistent with Hilliard's idea that "children, no matter what their racial or ethnic background, should be presented with pictures of the real world [because] that is how we can support accurate perception" (p. 99).

While teachers believe that their students all have equal potential to become scholars, regardless of their gender, color, family income, and prior experience in school, they do not assume that their students are the *same* or that they learn in the same way. Real practitioners in the major disciplines use many sources of information in addition to print, for example, maps, graphs, charts, timelines, films, photographs, interviews, oral histories, and observations. These sources bring alternative modalities to the learning process (Woodward, Baxter, & Robinson, 1999) and alternative ways for students to enter into investigations.

The emphasis on student talk is an expression of social equity joined with responsibility, in that each student has a voice and equal power in influencing and contributing to the thinking of the group. Another expression is the expectation that students will engage in community service through clubs and schoolwide drives. Regardless of a poverty background, students are not "needy" and, to the contrary, have something to contribute to their neighborhood. Many of the clubs involve service to the community. For example, students in a bicycle club learn to repair bicycles and make them available to inner-city St. Ellen children.

These core beliefs come together in the kind of student investigations that Potter's sixth graders are conducting in the cultures unit described in the opening vignette of this chapter. Students engage in scholarly inquiry as a learning community and use cross talk, dramatization of folk tales, and written reports as ways to bring each student's voice into constructing an understanding of what culture is. The translation of these beliefs and ideas about learning is by no means a carbon copy of another school's approach. The school history that follows tells the story, part struggle and part victory, of the school's unique formulation of a Schools for Thought approach to investigations.

CARTER-DEAN'S HISTORY AND THE EMERGENCE OF INVESTIGATIONS

"I can always tell people we were there when they gave birth to Schools for Thought, and step by step held each other's hands, and the crying and anxiety," recalls a pioneer teacher at Carter-Dean. "We made it," she continues. "And I think that when we look back, we are saying, Wow! *We did this!*"

Carter-Dean's signature practice—their particular, schoolwide approach to investigations—was forged in a crucible of desegregation and paradigm shifts in middle-grades education in St. Ellen. But the emergence of the model from that turmoil is only part of the story. Two other movements were emerging in the city and state—the inclusion of special education students and high-stakes testing—that would pose further challenges and contribute to the culture and character of the school's innovative investigative model. Desegregation, school–museum partnerships, applications of cognitive science to middle-grades learning, and transformations in special education are all a part of the unfolding story of how investigations became deeply rooted as the signature practice of Carter-Dean.

Desegregation Background

During the 1980s, St. Ellen was under court order to bring about racial balance in schools across the city. The state had maintained segregated schools for 115 years, much longer than in most southern states (Levins, 1994). The lawsuit that precipitated the St. Ellen school desegregation case was brought in 1972 by an African American mother who sued to keep her children in a vibrant middle-class school when overcrowding resulted in their being sent to an overcrowded school in a low-income, struggling neighborhood. The case languished over the next 10 years until a U.S. district judge took over the case, finding that many suburban communities were complicit in maintaining segregation policies. Under threat of court-ordered consolidation of all of the suburban school districts, local leaders negotiated a desegregation plan in 1982 that included transfers of Black inner-city students to suburban schools and the formation of magnet schools to bring suburban students into the city, to form, finally, racially balanced student bodies (Freivogel, 2001).

Magnet schools, a strategy for desegregation in St. Ellen and in cities across the country, were to have 60% black students and 40% White students, with a 5% deviation allowed. The magnet schools faced the challenge of creating high-quality programs that would rival the quality of suburban schools and attract and keep White suburban students. They got off to a slow start, with a withdrawal rate by White suburban students of 41%, with the long bus ride to the city cited as a problem. Nevertheless, the business community reported in 1995 that African American magnet students were graduating at twice the rate of African American students in non-magnet schools. Fifty-nine percent of the city's African American students were in desegregated schools in 1995, in contrast to 18% in 1980. Carter-Dean opened in 1996 in a context of integrated magnet schools that looked positive for African American students and faced challenges of sustaining suburban involvement (Freivogel, 2001).

The idea of a new middle school focused on student *thinking* began germinating in conversations among district leaders, teachers, and community leaders. Through the 1990s the idea grew and blossomed into a full school–museum–university partnership and a schoolwide model for learning—Schools for Thought—that was unique in St. Ellen and the country, and promised to be a sterling model of suburban–urban cooperation.

School and Museum Partnership

A science magnet school was the dream of several people as early as 1982, almost 15 years before Carter-Dean opened its doors. The president of the St. Ellen Science Center envisioned an intensive partnership between a science museum and an individual school that would reach deeply into the curriculum and daily learning—a novel idea that went beyond most museum education programs. When the Science Center director pushed this idea with the St. Ellen public schools, the James McDonnell Foundation, based in St. Ellen, gave a grant to the St. Ellen public schools and the Science Center to look at models together that would address the educational needs of children in the city district. Their first visit was to Buffalo, New York, home of the first museum school to form a partnership with a specific school. The Buffalo program fit the St. Ellen Science Center's philosophy of informal science learning and clarified the two-way benefit of the partnership. Students would have more access to science, and the museum would learn a lot about education.

An existing St. Ellen middle school called Madison Middle School was a candidate to become the incubator for the new magnet school because its enterprising principal, Alvera Williams, had already established lively connections with the Science Center, the St. Ellen Zoo, the Botanical Gardens, and a local Ecology Center. Madison teachers who became the "pioneer teachers" in the new school think that the planners chose Madison because of its commitment to innovation. Says Fran Hull, a Carter-Dean science specialist, "They looked at the teachers and saw a lot of excitement. And the children, when they came in, were excited." It helped that Madison was known to have the best attendance record for both teachers and students in the district.

Teachers Meet Researchers

In spring of 1993, with funding from the McDonnell Foundation, a Madison science teacher, another Madison administrative staff member, and a science center representative flew to Stanford, California, to meet with a renowned university scientist, the late Ann Brown, who was working on ways to apply cognitive learning theories to the classroom. McDonnell was funding several researchers to explore how to apply cognitive science to classroom learning. At the University of California, Ann Brown was developing the concept of "communities of learners" in elementary science classrooms (Brown & Campione, 1994). At Vanderbilt University, John Bransford was piloting the Jasper Series, a CD-ROM-based set of problem-solving and mathematics challenges embedded in the adventures of a bright and curious boy, Jasper Woodbury. At the Ontario Institute in Canada, Carl Bereiter and Marlene Scardemalia were developing computer environments in which students could pose questions and connect ideas. Other than having a common funder, these research projects were entirely separate before the St. Ellen planners brought them together in one school.

Brown and her colleagues' lack of pretension impressed the teachers. "They were *not* the big shots. They just sat down beside you talking to you. You wouldn't have known who they were," said one of the visiting Madison teachers. The visiting teachers tried out some of the science activities themselves in the California classroom. "We got to interact with the children; they were excited," recalls the Madison science teacher. Brown's group made the St. Ellen educators do the activities that the children were doing. "We turned out to be terrible failures at everything, particularly the science things. They [the children] kept pulling and showing me, and I didn't know what they were talking about, but it was interesting!"

Then the whole Madison staff of 24 teachers flew to Nashville to observe a classroom using the Jasper Woodbury series and have an inservice on curriculum design. The Jasper series fit the planners' early belief that most learning takes place in real situations rather than through abstract exercises. An appealing adolescent, Jasper provided those real situations and a character with whom students could identify. Nashville lent Madison starter units that were still under development. The Madison teachers came back animated, talking about how to apply the work of the California, Ontario, and Nashville researchers to design a curriculum for a new middle school.

Making a Model out of Chaos

The Madison teachers returned to St. Ellen with a harrowing deadline—their first weeklong summer school inservice training on the Schools for Thought concept with select, interested teachers at Madison and from a small number of other St. Ellen schools. These teachers would be piloting the approach in scattered classrooms for 2 years, starting in Fall 1993. Looking back to that spring and summer, Carter-Dean faculty who were a part of that beginning recall how consumed they were by anxiety. They felt almost overwhelmed by the challenge of integrating three powerful researchers' separate theories and practices, and their own experience and ideas into a coherent, whole-school model. Science specialist Hull recalls the pioneers' state of mind.

> There were three separate programs. We were shown things
> that were happening and we went to several [research] sites.
> But no one said, *"This is the plan."* It was exciting that you got
> to develop your own plan within those areas, but it was scary
> in that you didn't have anything to fall back on if it all crashed.
> *We were just out there!*

The teachers met at one another's houses during the spring, consuming pizzas over hours of talking. They had different thoughts on how things should be "as we continued to talk and talk and go to sleep and wake up and talk at midnight and call back the next day and reflect," says Aida Tannor, pioneer social studies teacher. How would they include parents in their plan for instruction? How would they select staff members who shared the same vision and philosophy? What elementary students in

Berkeley and Nashville were doing in 2 hours of their day was to be the grist for a full day of learning in St. Ellen's new middle school. "That's what the St. Ellen school was to be—a full middle school day, *a full year!*" They began to make decisions about what the curriculum would look like. "Teachers were excited, anxious; we wanted to know if we were moving in the right direction," Tannor recalls.

The Schools for Thought concept took shape slowly, with the idea of curriculum units organized around big topics and important questions, and a cycle of investigative strategies: posing a compelling topic, generating questions for investigation, learning research strategies, and sharing information. In Fall 1993, teachers intensified their earlier, tentative approach to inquiry. They began to interview outside teachers for the new school, and excitement rose. "The enthusiasm was just rising as we heard teaching candidates say, 'Oh, yes. *That's* what I'm looking for,'" says Hull.

During that first pilot year, the McDonnell Foundation stepped in again with resources by providing a postdoctoral fellowship to Audrey Cohen, a young graduate student of Marlene Scardamalia's at Ontario Institute, to observe and coach teachers in their nascent practices for a Schools for Thought approach. Cohen won the trust of Madison teachers through her informal yet respectful manner and her bubbling excitement about the teaching at Madison. Tannor describes having Cohen observe her class.

> We didn't know which door she was going to come in. Audrey being Audrey, wanting to catch everything just going on as usual, not anything staged, she came in the back door. She noticed that the classroom set up was basically small groups. Students were helping each other; I was piloting a textbook and doing that while students worked together. They were helping each other teach. They teach each other and only consult me if they have a question that no one in the group can answer. We were all doing what she was looking for. She was looking for teachers who were willing to make a change.

Cohen helped with the first curriculum unit designs and served as the first Schools for Thought coordinator in the school—a position closely linked with the Science Center, which Carter-Dean eventually picked up in its own budget.

Paradigm Shift

A year later, in 1994, Madison conducted a full pilot with more staff and 250 students. Title I students participated fully in the classroom with the Title I teacher, a first step toward an inclusive and academically diverse classroom. Although the teachers "felt good" about what they had done, not everyone then at the school was on board yet. A host of problems arose: reluctance of regular education teachers to take on responsibilities for students with disabilities, scheduling enough time for curriculum design, and the presence of teachers who, despite the whole-school commitment to Schools for Thought, continued to teach by lecturing. Principal Williams calls this "paradigm paralysis"—teachers feeling caught between old and new ways of teaching and working with one another.

Nevertheless, 2 years later, in the spring before the Fall 1996 opening of the new school beside the Science Center, a reporter from a national education journal visited the school and documented intensive, community-based investigations in full swing. An article with the headline, "Mix and Match: The Experimental Schools for Thought Combines Three Promising Cognitive Learning Approaches to Promote Deep and True Understanding," began as follows:

> Perched atop laboratory stools, eight students in Fran Hull's 7th grade science class are swapping notes about their field trip the previous day to a local steam-heating plant. "The Ashley street plant has been operating since 1988," says a small blond girl. "It was called a trash energy facility, but at the time, there were a lot of problems with environmental systems." Another student volunteers that the pipes carrying water to the plant are 22 miles long and two feet in diameter. So the conversation goes, with each student offering another scrap of information. Each time someone speaks, heads bend and students scribble intently in their notebooks. Along the way, the group discusses the "opacity" of smoke, the mathematics of converting water to steam, and the three forms of oxygen. Upon completing a thought, pupils call on classmates to take up the discussion. Their teacher sits silently, her arms folded across her chest, and takes it all in. (Viadero, 1996)

In Fall 1996, Carter-Dean Middle School opened in a new building beside the Science Center, with 510 students. The school opened with the first curriculum units designed by teachers and Science Center experts.

Looking back on the first 4 years of the new school, the pioneer teachers say that having to work through every issue in founding the school set down a pattern of cooperative problem solving that has persisted in the culture of the school. "Out of chaos came understanding, and that understanding led to creativity in the way we still resolve or solve issues," says Hull. Every time a problem comes up, teachers feel that they look for ways to work it out. "If there is a problem with scheduling, we work on it in committees; if teachers are trying to work out a discipline concern, we work with that together. We get a better understanding from the chaos and confusion."

Students with Disabilities in Investigations

During the Spring 1993 visit to Ann Brown's lab school at Stanford, Carter-Dean's program coordinator, Carla Wine, watched a fourth and a fifth grader expertly demonstrate a science project using diagrams, videotapes, and their own explanations. A California teacher explained that 7 months previously, the fifth grader, articulate and excited in the demonstration, entered the program unable to speak because of emotional and learning disabilities. "Yet this little boy was fluent, and I was impressed. I was impressed by the talk, and even more impressed by the student's demonstration," says Wine. That experience clinched Wine's own personal resolve to fully include students with disabilities in Carter-Dean classrooms.

From the beginning of planning the new school, Alvera Williams envisioned students with disabilities fully included in investigations. She enlisted a university faculty member to translate the behaviorist special education foundations then in place in the district into constructivist approaches. This report was used at the 1996 summer institute to train the new Carter-Dean faculty. Given the challenge of the investigative model itself, focusing on students with disabilities was too much for some of them. "Some teachers were furious and acted out," recalls a pioneer teacher. "They complained that 'nobody told me how to do inclusion.'"

The school opened with 20 students with disabilities fully included and 10 in a substantially separate classroom, a situation that the principal viewed as a compromise. Some parents were concerned that students who had "grown up" in separate elementary classrooms would be overwhelmed by the regular classroom. Eager for the school to be successful in a district still ardently resisting full inclusion, the district special education coordinator argued that some of the 10 separate students could be phased in to the investigative classrooms and some could stay for more sheltered learning. The two special education teachers worked mainly within the classrooms, supporting students with disabilities as they worked with students of varied abilities in their pod. The special education teachers rotated among the content-area classrooms as the special educator and grade-level team decided would be most useful.

MAKING INVESTIGATIONS WORK FOR ALL

In many schools, rigorous research projects are reserved for honors students and children designated "gifted and talented"; at Carter-Dean, investigations are the bread of everyday learning. The active participation of such an academically diverse body of students and students' high marks on statewide tests do not just happen, however. Several features of the Schools for Thought model make investigations inclusive and supportive of students with different experiences, academic abilities and disabilities, and economic and cultural backgrounds. These elements include the following:

1. *Interdisciplinary units* provide a predictable structure for investigations.
2. *Cooperative structures* build student voice and facilitate adult support.
3. *Technology tools* scaffold inquiry and writing.
4. Faculty members share the teaching of *literacy skills* for investigations.
5. Classroom *assessment systems* reward cooperative investigation.

The challenge that is ever present in learning at Carter-Dean is how students can explore and discover knowledge about big social/scientific questions that could result in divergent learning outcomes, while also directly acquiring information and concepts identified as "standards" in the state frameworks and assessment. Separately and together, the elements of Carter-Dean's investigations bring challenges that require constant vigilance and learning on the part of staff. The positive results for students in the school can be attributed to the interplay of the above five elements.

Interdisciplinary Units

All learning at Carter-Dean takes the form of investigations within interdisciplinary curriculum units. Teachers, including content teachers, special education staff, and curriculum specialists from the Science Center, work together by grade level and design units for sixth, seventh, and eighth graders. Usually students complete two to three units each year. Teachers design units during the summer and after school with the help of their science specialist from the Science Center and other support they draw from museums, surrounding universities, and community organizations. Focused on compelling topics and big questions, the units integrate, in a systematic way, many curriculum practices the teachers observed at Stanford and Nashville, and target information and concepts that they identified in the state learning standards.

Figure 4.2 is a simplified description of a sixth-grade unit on the environment, drawn from detailed written curriculum materials for each of the content areas (science, social studies, mathematics, literature). The unit,

Figure 4.2. Excerpt from Curriculum Unit Plan: The Earth, Environment, and Me

Phase	Science	Social studies	Literature	Mathematics
Big idea/ principle	People impact the changing environment and the changing environment impacts people.			
	Misconceptions to be dispelled: (1) Man-made changes always have a negative impact on the environment. (2) All living things are vastly different. (3) All environmental problems are man-made. (4) The law is made for some people and not others.			
State standards	Characteristics and interactions of living organisms Processes and interactions of earth's biosphere, atmosphere, lithosphere, and hydrosphere Changes in ecosystems Scientific inquiry processes	Legal systems and how they are organized Why people have established legal systems Relationships of individuals to the law and legal systems	Determine an author's purpose Summarize a work of literature Demonstrate an ability to compare and contrast Understand and use conventions in writing	Analysis of environmental data Reasoning about numbers Understanding probability Reading graphs and charts of environmental data Looking for patterns and relationships
Anchor	Students view and respond to the video: *The Earth and Me*			
Dilemma, sample research questions, problems	*Dilemma:* Do people change the environment or does the environment change people?			

How does water get polluted? Does pollution hurt you? What are good changes in the environment? When is a change an ecological disaster? What are some environmental issues within the state? *Sample problem:* How can pollution destroy a forest?	How does culture affect the way people use land? Do all people have certain human rights? What rights? Who protects our rights? Who can change the law? How does the court system work? What is an expert witness? *Sample problem:* How can people cause dust? When is it good? When is it a disaster?	How can literature show conflicts between people and their environments? How can an author describe an environment? How is the environment affecting the character? How are dogs different from wolves? *Sample problem:* How does Henry Casey adapt to the environment in *White Fang*?	How does the profit motive affect people's choices in using the environment? What kind of environmental data can we show in graphs and charts? What are statistics? How can they help us understand pollution? *Sample problem:* What factors could cause the fish population in our tank to grow?
Benchmark mini-lessons (related to state standards) Characteristics of living organisms Atmospheric layers and their functions Causes of pollution Positive and negative change in the environment Scientific inquiry processes Scientific notation	Features and purposes of legal systems How pollution laws are made How courts work Making arguments for both sides of an issue Using graphs and charts to present information Local environmental issues	Ways to determine the author's purpose Inferring conflict in literature Summarizing a literary text Comparing and contrasting characters Cause and effect relationships Using capitalization Using commas in a series	Making predictions based on probabilities Constructing and interpreting data displays Applying number theory concepts Using estimation strategies Looking for patterns in data displays

Figure 4.2. (continued)

Resources	World Wide Web (Internet), CD-ROM, laserdisc, videodisc, other electronic materials, related field experiences, guest speakers, reference books, content-area books, research papers, ERIC documents, CSILE/Knowledge Forum
Field experiences	Science Center, Botanical Garden, Tyson Research Center, Big Map (St. Ellen Science Center Living Exhibit), Springboard to Learning, Old Courthouse, Bar Association, Ultra Light Club, Melvin Price Lock and Dam
Knowledge sharing ("test your ideas")	Once our pod research is complete, students will create new jigsaw groups with one person from each research group acting as the expert within the newly formed group. The new jigsaw groups will then begin the process of completing the consequential tasks and share their knowledge. They also may cross talk about their research, and share their knowledge, diagrams, and plans. Each research category is a piece needed to complete the consequential task.
Consequential tasks ("going public")	1. Write an essay to answer your research group's question.
	2. Conduct a court case on industrial pollution: Students will apply their new knowledge and understanding to decide if the SYNCO Corp. (fictitious corporation) is guilty or innocent of an ecological disaster that destroyed hundreds of miles of ecosystem, killed thousands of species of plants and animals, caused major health problems, and presented frightening future implications for generations to come. A jury will find SYNCO guilty or innocent of alleged crimes, based on evidence presented at the trial. All parties involved will prepare a case (including opening and closing remarks) and defend or prosecute by using witnesses. The jury will discuss the merits of the case and render a verdict. The simulation is based on a recent event: a similar prosecution of a local company.
Assessments	1. *Pre/posttest of environmental knowledge*
	2. *Investigations*: Students will identify problems and define their scope and elements, develop and apply strategies in preventing and solving problems, and evaluate the extent to which the strategies address the problems. Before beginning the investigation, students will write what they already know about each research question. Near the end of the unit, students will rewrite those answers and compare notes.
	3. *Pod self-assessment* and individual assessment using rubrics and point system provided by the teachers
	4. *Teacher assessment* of student effort, participation, and knowledge in the trial

titled "The Earth, Environment, and Me," follows a 3-week orientation to the school. Incoming sixth-grade students work on this unit for 12 weeks, followed in the spring by the world cultures unit featured in the opening vignette of this chapter. Like all units in the school, the environment unit has a consistent structure that includes each of the following phases:

The big idea. This idea or "principle" will generate the questions and activities for the unit. In this unit, the idea is that people and the environment affect one another.

State standards. Teachers agree on a set of standards from each of the four main subject areas that will focus the investigation. For example, in science, the standards are related to the interactions of organisms and of the different levels of the earth's atmosphere; in social studies, they are related to legal systems and whether and how they regulate people's interactions with the environment.

Anchor. Teachers arouse students' interest in the big idea through a powerful experience, often a related OMNIMAX film at the Science Center. For this unit they view *The Blue Planet*, a space film about the Earth filmed aboard several space shuttle missions. Volcanoes, earthquakes, and typhoons are visible, but it is the signs of pollution, ozone depletion, deforestation, and energy consumption as seen from space that reveal the more disturbing impact of humans.

Dilemma and questions. Teachers identify a big conflict and generate questions in each content area that students can investigate. The science questions might include, How does water get polluted? A literature question might ask, How can literature show conflicts between people and their environments? While students generate their own questions after the anchor and considerable reading, these questions reflect teachers' advance thinking about the topic and prepare them to hear students' questions. Students later work in small groups and select questions for study.

Benchmark mini-lessons. Teachers identify concepts, skills, and background information, often those in the state standards, that they will directly teach to support the investigations. The social studies teacher will do a mini-lesson on how courts work, as a foundation for students' understanding of pollution cases; the mathematics teacher, a mini-lesson on analyzing data in emissions charts.

Resources and field experiences. The school, Internet, and broader community provide students multiple ways to gather information for an investigation.

Knowledge sharing. Sharing takes place throughout the investigative cycle, with cross talk a major strategy for sharing. An on-line program called Knowledge Forum, described further below, gives students a place to connect ideas across the grade level. A student says, "If we can understand from our friends, we might understand it better." Students also use performances (e.g., the dramatization of a folk tale in the world cultures unit) to share what they are learning.

Consequential tasks. These tasks require students to pull together their learning in an essay or collaborative activity, which is an important part of their evaluation and grading. In "The Earth, Environment, and Me" unit (see Figure 4.2), students write both an individual essay on a question related to pollution and take part in a mock court trial of a company that is being sued for exceeding regulated emission standards.

Assessments. Evaluation of student learning outcomes takes several forms in a unit. A final grade may take into account pre/postassessments, self-assessments by members of a pod, individual self-assessments, and teacher assessments.

This consistent unit structure spawns a language of inquiry that belongs to every person in the school. In the principal's conference room, visitors see a poster that students see every day in their classrooms. It is titled "Glossary" and defines all the words that are strange to a newcomer but part of everyday talk for Carter-Dean students: anchor, consequential task, cooperative learning, cross talk, Knowledge Forum, rotations, and other key terms that encode the Schools for Thought model. The glossary is a constant reminder that the school's philosophy and practices belong to everyone and that they hold a unique and shared meaning for everyone in the school.

In the sixth-grade unit on the environment, outlined in Figure 4.2, students conducted a mock trial as a consequential unit task and assessment activity. The SYNCO trial was named after a polluting company that was a defendant in an actual court case in St. Ellen that got extensive media coverage the previous year. Teachers thought up the mock trial as a way to introduce new Carter-Dean students to the kinds of real environmental challenges being fought out in the courts. The trial also requires them to bring together the information they are learning about the social, legal, and scientific aspects of pollution cases. The excerpt from field observations that follows points up how much new learning and preparation this simulation requires of students, including court roles and procedures, technical terms related to pollution standards, chemistry of pollution, ways of organizing data, and issues that can frame a pollution case.

"Courtroom will come to order." A scowling teacher sits in the role of judge at a raised desk in front, while groups of students are milling around on both sides, preparing to take the roles of counsels and witnesses for the defense and prosecution. The sixth-grade science teacher assists from the side, occasionally quieting the students in the "audience." Students settle down as the counsel (C) for the prosecution, a tall African American girl, holds note cards as she questions a witness (W) for the defense—a very slight White boy with bright red hair—about the impact of the coal used by the company. The clerk calls for a reading of emission standards, and a witness from the EPA comes forward and reads the standards for SYNCO Power. The counsel for the prosecution begins questioning a witness, then the defense counsel (D) objects to the line of questioning.

> C: Do you know what type of coal SYNCO burns?
> W: Yes.
> C: Cheapest form of coal?
> W: Yes.
> C: What kind of coal?
> W: Bituminous.
> C: What kind of chemical does it [give off]?
> W: After it is burned or before?
> D: Objection.
> *Judge:* He should have this background knowledge, so keep quiet!
> [firmly]
> C: After it is burned.
> W: Sulfur dioxide.
> C: No further questions.

The defense counsel rises with a chart that shows diminished emissions at the plant. He extracts from the witness the information that SYNCO has used new technologies to actually reduce the emissions of sulfur dioxide from burning coal.

The trial proceeds at a very slow pace over the first 2 days because students have much to learn about court procedures and about the details of the pollution issues they are arguing. At one point, the science teacher almost falls asleep, but she wakes quickly to continue patient coaching with the novice lawyers and witnesses. But attention picks up on the third day as students understand the procedures better and hone their arguments.

Students currently in the audience watch courtroom questioning that they have seen only on TV, if at all. The students who are on the witness stand struggle with how to enact their role and stop frequently to consult their notes for points they had planned to make.

In addition to requiring them to use new content knowledge, the unit also acculturates these new sixth-grade students into being "scholars" at Carter-Dean, a word they often hear from teachers. They know they have to talk about their thinking, that they can take their time learning and saying things, and that people are expected to listen to their ideas and generally will be respectful. Consistent with the school's belief that student scholars need to search out the truth of what is happening in their society, they are learning surprising and sometimes shocking things about their world and their community, for example, that a company knowingly might pollute a city's environment.

Cooperative Structures

A second element of Carter-Dean investigations that makes them accessible to all students is the structures that support students in learning from one another. In many traditional classrooms, where students are expected to work individually and quietly, students with disabilities and students with weak background knowledge and skills may struggle along on their own. At Carter-Dean, investigations are small-group endeavors that provide each student a sheltered and highly structured context for active learning. Two main cooperative structures are pods, which help students learn from one another, and rotations, which facilitate adult support to the students who need it most.

Pods. Throughout a unit, small groups of four or five students work together and assume responsibility for an important piece of the investigation. Pods have a number of specific features that make them different from some informal small groups.

- The pods take on a piece of the larger group investigation, a specific question or set of questions within the larger class topic, and its members are responsible for bringing back what they learn to the whole class.
- A pod usually works together throughout the unit and stays together in each subject area. Sometimes they are regrouped for mathematics.
- They are the "first resort" when an individual has a question. Pod members can call on the teacher only if they cannot find the

answer themselves. At this point, the question belongs not to the individual but to the pod. This gives students with disabilities strong peer models, peer and teacher support, and leadership opportunities (Morocco, Walker, & Lewis, 2003).

- Pods are usually heterogeneous. Students with disabilities occasionally are placed in one pod for special assistance, but mainly students with disabilities are dispersed among the pods.
- The pod is responsible for all students' learning; the students' evaluation and grade rest on how well students work and learn as a group.

For students who are reluctant to speak out in classroom cross talk, the pod is a protected context for conversation. Potter, the sixth-grade teacher from the opening vignette of this chapter, explains:

> In a pod they are likely to have a voice, to speak, and to feel more secure about where they are because they work every day with these same students. It gives them more comfort with the peers around them. [They learn that] with politeness, with respect, that you treat someone the way you want to be treated. That gives them a confidence, a trust, that when they do speak they are not going to be ridiculed, that they will be listened to, that even if they are wrong it is going to be okay.

Team-building activities over the course of the year promote each student's ability to be a risk-taker in his or her pod, and to work together. An eighth grader who is in the school band says pods are like band: "In pods you have to work together and in bands you have to work together." A seventh-grade girl says that the teachers put them together to learn because "it teaches you about the real world" where smart people and slower people won't be separated.

> When you are in the real world you are going to be working with people who have higher academics and people who maybe aren't as smart as you. Sometimes you get stuck in a pod where there's either people who are a lot smarter than you or people who don't want to do anything, not that they don't know what they are supposed to do . . . so it's kind of hard.

They also understand that what you learn in the pod has to be shared with the whole class. "They say it's like pods, but it's really the class, because after you learn stuff with your pod, you have to discuss it with the whole class. That's what we do in math all the time. Every day we [the pod] have to talk with the class."

Another image from the world cultures unit points out how a pod may support a student with disabilities (Morocco, Walker, & Lewis, 2003). Four students from one pod, Eric, Jillian, Amber, and Diana, sit together on the floor outside their classroom to rehearse a scene from a read-aloud they will perform for their class. Jillian has specific disabilities that affect her reading and writing, attention to learning activities, and information processing, and is quieter than the other three. Their text is an African folk tale, "He-Lion." In the story, He-Lion thinks overly well of himself and dominates the other animals in the forest.

Reviewing the book, Amber realizes, "We *gotta* have animals!" Amber agrees that they need to take the parts of different animals and suggests that Eric should be the lion. She draws Jillian into the negotiation over parts and asks which animal she would like to read. Jillian agrees to read the rabbit's part, and they begin rehearsing. When it is time for Jillian to read her lines, she is silent. Eric leans over and points to her lines, saying quietly and in a reassuring tone, "It's your turn."

Task rotation. Peer support is important but not sufficient for students who struggle with limited background knowledge and independent learning skills. Task rotations are designed to put teacher assistance where it is most needed. Three or four activities take place concurrently in a classroom, requiring different levels of teacher support. When a pod completes one task (e.g., reading reference materials for its research question), it rotates immediately to the next task on the rotation schedule for the pod (e.g., a vocabulary exercise). A chart assigning pods to activities is always posted on the board. As a result, students are never waiting or unsure about what to do next; as soon as they complete one activity, they progress to the next. The rotation system allows content teachers, special education teachers, and aides to circulate to observe students' work and to provide assistance to pods as needed. It also enables students to share materials.

Figure 4.3 is the rotation chart for the week in which students are preparing dramatizations of "He-Lion" and other fables. On Day III, two pods work on their own preparing their fable presentations, two get direct teacher assistance with revising and editing their final paper for the unit, two reread and choose a fable, and two work on an independent "game" teaching them synonyms and antonyms. Extended classes over 50 minutes are likely to work through three to four rotations in a day.

While the rotation system frees the teacher to rotate among pods and contribute help where needed, it keeps students building specific skills and vocabulary related to the ongoing investigation.

Figure 4.3. Rotation Schedule for World Cultures Lessons

Rotation	Day I	Day II	Day III	Day IV
Reread and select fable	1 & 2	3 & 4	5 & 6	—
Rehearse fable presentation	—	1 & 2	3 & 4	5 & 6
Finish cultures paper	3 & 4	5 & 6	—	1 & 2
Synonyms/antonyms	5 & 6	—	1 & 2	3 & 4

Jigsaw. The curriculum units are designed around very big questions and dilemmas, and an extensive set of narrower questions. In the jigsaw, each pod takes responsibility for investigating one or two questions, then pods reconstitute so that each student is in a new group with students from 4 or 5 other pods. As in the classic jigsaw strategy (Johnson, Johnson, & Holubek 1994), each student takes a turn teaching the new group what he or she has been learning. Knowing that they will have to teach others motivates students to participate actively in their pod and tells them that their pod work is important. Jigsaws encourage students to share and discuss ideas, and can lead to students synthesizing the information and ideas with which they are grappling.

Technology Tools

Technology makes investigations accessible to students with learning difficulties, weak background knowledge, and limited reading experience. Some of the intellectual support roles that technology plays include the following.

Motivate students to engage in an extended study of a topic. Films in the OMNIMAX theater of the Science Center launch many of the units. Stunning visuals make unfamiliar topics like Alaska and the Earth's surface accessible and gripping. Students want to know more and begin asking questions that lead them into the material and concepts in the unit.

Provide information to investigate questions. For each unit, the teachers approve a set of Web addresses that have useful and potentially reliable information about the unit dilemma. For the sixth-grade environment unit, the science teacher announces that she got the address of the Coalition for the Environment and the Environmental Protection Association. Teachers also include addresses that will inform students about social action on behalf of the environment and encourage them to be "activist" researchers. "I was on the Web last night and found a whole lot of activist links." CD-ROM discs provide visual and print databases.

Embed analytic and problem-solving skills in a real context. Teachers pull in the CD-ROM-based Adventures of Jasper Woodbury to anchor a dilemma or teach mathematics and problem-solving skills, such as ratio and proportion, time/distance, and measurement. Students identify with young Jasper and love to solve the problems that arise in his adventures. Another example is Sim City, an award-winning city planning simulation that enables students to design a city and discuss issues of zoning, architecture, traffic control, and other challenges during their study of how St. Ellen compares with selected other cities in the world.

Provide drafting, revising, and editing tools. It is not surprising at Carter-Dean to see seventh graders writing eight- or nine-page papers about what they have learned. Students with writing difficulties stay in class at one of the nine computers there; others work in the library with its bank of many additional computers. Teachers move quietly behind students as they compose on the computer, as in these interactions between the seventh-grade social studies teacher and a girl with learning disabilities during the final week of the pollution unit.

> "Can you read that wonderful concluding paragraph to the class, Dora?" Tannor has just read the ending of Dora's essay over her shoulder as Dora revises at the computer. Dora reads the last paragraph and the teacher repeats one of the sentences: "Do you hear that? 'Without the environment giving us what we need, there will be no *us*'" [her emphasis]. Tannor repeats the line slowly and emphatically before going on to have another student read part of his essay. Dora continues to work at the computer, making revisions based on suggestions from her pod, her teacher, and her parents (she had taken the essay home to read to them). She changes "amount of pollution" to "level of pollution" and "inasant" to "innocent." Then she uses the spelling checker.

Parents have a set of editing marks that the school gives them for when their children bring home an essay for their reaction.

Help students connect questions and findings. Knowledge Forum is the most innovative use of technology in the school. A contribution of the Ontario Institute, this software formalizes and facilitates students' sharing of the questions, ideas, and conclusions that emerge over their long pod and classwide investigations. A class enters the sets of questions it is studying into a web of questions for the entire grade level. Individual students and pods enter ideas and "solutions" as the investigations proceed. Because computers are networked with one another across the school, students from other classes in the grade level can open the web and add in their own ideas and questions.

One impact of Knowledge Forum is that students become used to stepping back to think about what they are learning and they take it for granted that knowledge is shared and developed in a community of learners. The Knowledge Forum helps the teacher by making students' thinking visible for conversation and refinement. Between the Forum and students' extended essays at the end of most units, students write and think about their learning a great deal.

Access to all of the various technologies for learning at the neighboring Science Center and these in-school tools makes Carter-Dean unique. Teachers live with technology in many forms and are comfortable with it, because students use these tools regularly in every unit and content area. Students take it for granted as part of their learning environment.

These technology tools for investigations spill over into after-school clubs. In a club for building websites, students are working on the question, How did slaves escape to safe states? They have been researching slavery on the Internet and have put several stories on their website. Under the history of St. Ellen, students have posted one story about a slave named Henry Box Brown, who escaped from the students' own state to Philadelphia by traveling 26 hours in a box that was 2 feet 8 inches deep, 2 feet wide, and 3 feet long. Another story is about Ellen Craft, a light-skinned woman who cropped her hair and disguised herself as a White man leading her "slave" (her husband William) to freedom. Another tells of how Harriet Tubman, through 19 trips back to the south, helped free at least 300 fellow captives.

They chose the specific topic of the Underground Railroad because the ancestors of several of the African American students in the club were slaves, and because their state was a slave state bordering Illinois, which was free. The teacher comments that "in many ways, St. Ellen is still a border, and lots of the issues are going on today." Consistent with the school's beliefs about what social equity means, the students are using technology tools to uncover hard truths about their own ancestry and the history of their own state.

Shared Teaching of Literacy Skills

In most schools, the role of teaching literacy skills belongs to the language arts teacher. Carter-Dean does not have a designated "language arts" teacher and expects all teachers to share the role of teaching students the literacy skills that they need for investigations. Investigations require that students read and understand a wide variety of print, on-line, and oral "texts" and connect the information from those texts. They are expected to write, with correct spelling and conventions, extended essays about their research. And they are expected to be able to articulate their thinking to others. Students vary dramatically in these literacy skills, and all teachers in all content areas have the responsibility of teaching these skills. All teachers develop mini-lessons around grammar, writing and editing conventions, and vocabulary development. Lessons develop from authentic work, rather than page-to-page language arts and spelling textbooks.

While some teachers use rote methods to teach these skills, many try to use challenging games, with the goal of making students think. As an example, a seventh-grade literature teacher teaches personal, possessive, and indefinite pronouns by having students compose group stories. Each pod is given a poster with a topic and lead sentence, followed by the challenge of writing second and third sentences that adhere to the story begun in the lead sentence and use more than one pronoun correctly. They underline the pronoun then rotate to the next table to add to the story of another group. Field notes offer a snapshot of this pronoun lesson in progress.

A pod with the topic, "music," has the lead sentence, "Everyone at the concert was clapping and dancing." The group stands around the poster suggesting ideas for next sentences. When a student suggests that they add, "They were there when someone got shot," another pod member objects that the sentence is not about the topic of music. Another student rephrases the sentence to include music: "We could say, 'During the dancing, someone got shot.'" A different student objects to bringing in the idea of someone getting shot, "That's not about music!"

Another pod, with the initial topic, "newspaper," has the lead, "Our team has won their last four games. Our pitcher threw several strikeouts." The students add, "After every game the band played." When someone points out that they need to include a pronoun, they change the sentence to "Everyone celebrated while the band played," and underline the pronoun.

The activity is complete when each pod has circulated to each poster and returned to its original table to read aloud the finished "stories" to the class. Consistent with the school's belief that learning needs to be challenging and situated in real experiences, the activity integrates pronoun use with other literacy skills. The students are required to elaborate text, compose connected sentences, attend to grammatical features, read silently and aloud, and pronounce words correctly. And in this intellectually challenging context, students have fun.

Content teachers tend to see teaching the specialized vocabulary of a content area as a part of literacy. Even the "allied arts" teachers of home economics say, "Just like there is a language of mathematics, students have to learn and use symbols related to sewing." In giving students a quiz on information about volcanoes, a science teacher calls attention to the use of metaphoric language in the specialized science terms.

> *T:* Why are the shield volcanoes so named?
> *S1:* A shield volcano hardens up around the outside of it.
> *T:* What's the hole [of the volcano] like? [Pushing for a more precise answer]
> *S2:* [He gives same guess.] A shield volcano hardens up around the outside.

Other students try to figure out the use of "shield."

> *S3:* It's called shield because the opening where the lava comes out *looks* like a shield.

When the students stumble on the literal meaning behind the term *igneous*, she directs them to its Latin root.

> *S1:* The three types are igneous, sedimentary, and . . .
> *T:* The word *igneous* means?
> *S2:* Large?
> *S1:* Rock?
> *S3:* The mother's rock?
> *T:* This will be on the test. *Ignis* in Latin means "fire."

This same teacher later coaches a class in how to apply the state writing standards to sample essays; content teachers are all helping with this preparation that day. The students automatically use cross talk routines in discussing problems with the writing samples.

T: We can pull out our papers. Look at your rubrics and see why
      he got a 1. [Reads the rubric aloud.] What do we mean by
      mechanical error?
S1: Not having "ed," "ing," or apostrophes.
T: William, please read the first example. [He reads aloud.] Who
      can identify some of the problems?
William: He didn't have a period. I pass to Wendy.
Wendy: He does not capitalize. I pass to . . .
T: That's enough, let's go to 2. [Miranda reads aloud.] Paper tends
      to ramble. What does that mean?
S2: Sentence goes on and on and does not stop.
T: It keeps on going and going. We understand irrelevant details
      [smiles at her own remark], don't we?

Assessment Systems

Carter-Dean teachers feel that they and their students continually are
assessing their learning. Some of the units in some content areas include
extended, teacher-designed pre/posttests of content knowledge in multiple
choice form. All use a combination of assessment strategies: cross talk,
examining students' drafts, observing their pod work, and assessing consequential tasks. Both the pod and the individual are responsible for what
students learn and receive points for the quality of their work. Students
receive an assessment guide at the beginning of each unit that specifies the
basis for their unit grade. Figure 4.4 outlines the number of points assigned
to each required activity of the world cultures unit, "Myths, Legends, and
Folk Tales." The guide is not a rubric related to quality but a listing of the
different kinds of learning that are important in the unit.

A teacher explains that students differ in how they can best express
their understanding, so it's only fair that grading take into account many
kinds of activities: homework, journals, pod work, skills work, final essays,
final tests, and other activities. Other content-area teachers will have similar but content-specific guides for grading. Both students and teacher sign
off on the students' scores for each aspect of this investigation. In other
units, such as the sixth-grade environment unit, teachers may distribute
the points differently.

The use of cross talk for ongoing reflection and assessment is probably the most unusual aspect of the unit assessment system. Cross talk
pushes students to reflect throughout the investigation on how their learning is going. It makes visible to the teacher the students' thinking and their
misconceptions, for example, Kinesha's implication in the opening vignette
of the chapter that Kente cloth is general to all of Africa rather than being

Figure 4.4. Unit III: Myths, Legends, and Folk Tales—Literature Scoring Guide

Unit Activities	Possible points	Your points
Daily homework assignments completed	20	_____
Daily journal entries completed	20	_____
Quizzes (2 @ 5 points, 1 pod quiz, 10 points)	20	_____
Posttest on plot and theme	30	_____
Classwork	20	_____
Peer assessment: Participates, follows instructions, uses pod rules	10	_____
Writing Renegades Skills work completed	20	_____
Research paper on your chosen culture	30	_____
Consequential task: Write a folk tale or myth, individual project	20	_____
Group presentation of one folk tale from your pod	10	_____
Group presentation of *Bruh Rabbit*	20	_____
Fourth independent book project, due May 10 or May 11	30	_____
Final unit test	100	_____

Total possible points	350	A = 322–350
Your total points	_____	B = 280–321
Your grade	_____	C = 245–279
		D = 210–244
		F = 209 and below

part of a specific African culture. Cross talk is a favorite way to conclude a class. Toward the end of one class, after each pod had completed its rotations for the day, Potter asks her students to think about what went well for them that class. She launches directly into cross talk with a question, "What went well today? I pass to Stephanie." Several students comment, passing to one another: "People were talking but I still got some work done." "I didn't think I would get a good grade but I did." "I was wrong to be talking during the math work, but the good thing is that I passed the math quiz and I got help." "I got stuck on page 114 and didn't understand."

"Good: I understood the worksheets. Bad: didn't pass the test but maybe the next time." The teacher concludes this 2-minute reflection with, "Thank you for your statements. It *lifts me* on this rainy day. We too much tend to focus on the negative."

Potter is convinced that cross talk at the end of a unit reveals understandings that students do not express in their essays or other culminating tasks. Discussing the cross talk on cultures with her student teacher afterward, Potter said she was "surprised at how much they had recalled."

> The research papers didn't even show as much as they were showing in the cross talk. One student would bring up a topic, say clothing, or color, or religion, and that seemed to spark ideas in the others. They don't necessarily write down what they know, but once they are in that group and talking, they really do talk about what they have learned.

In hearing the cross talk, she felt certain for the first time that all the work of visiting the art museum, reading, and searching on the Internet had been worthwhile.

LEADERSHIP CHALLENGES AND CHANGES

Balancing Inquiry Learning and High-Stakes Testing

State assessments were piloted in all cities, including St. Ellen, in 1998, the year that the first cohort of Carter-Dean students was in eighth grade. The test was implemented across the state in 1999, with a mandate that all schools move 10% of their students who scored in the first quintile that year to the second quintile by the next year, and that 10% of students in the fourth quintile move to the fifth. At the opening of Chapter 1, Carter-Dean principal Alvera Williams voiced the dilemma that increasing pressures from the district have posed for her school. As is her style, Williams took the problem to her teachers to solve. They brainstormed as a whole faculty and decided on several new steps to make their students more successful on statewide tests. For the first time in 2003–04, they engaged in practice periods for the test, but called them "academic practice," and designed materials to support these practice periods.

The faculty analyzed the previous year's test results to pinpoint errors and trained one another in setting formal lesson objectives to target highly specific, isolated skills. The teachers worked across content areas, whether or not the skill was domain-specific. They made the lessons as thought-provoking as possible, as the teacher did in the pronoun lesson described above. They developed a related packet of materials for parents to use with their children at home and gave out the materials at a special PTO meeting. Another strategy, which was painful for the whole faculty, was to give up their club time.

The sacrifice, from the faculty point of view, was that they used a 45-minute club period for the test preparation three times a week, where every adult in the school met with a small group of students on compelling literacy-related activities. (Williams ran a coveted Mystery Stories club.) After academic practice was instituted, the faculty saw students improve their ability to explain their answers in the ways required on state tests and they could see benefits to the extra work. Yet, the pain of compromising her philosophy is apparent in Williams's reluctance to focus on specific skills in isolation from investigations. As quoted in Chapter 1, she said, "'Til I take my last breath, that's truly how I believe learning takes place. This pulling out of a piece, it doesn't stay. The teaching–learning process is a natural outgrowth of a big idea, and you explore the idea in an integrated fashion." Yet, for the survival of the school and her own survival as its leader, she and her staff integrated direct instruction for test preparation into their yearlong investigations.

Maintaining this balance between more open-ended outcomes of investigative learning and the narrow content outcomes of statewide testing will be a continuing challenge for Williams and her faculty. One critical factor will be how much support she receives from district staff, including the special education leadership, as pressures to meet state and local targets intensify.

Making Investigative Learning Work for Students with Disabilities

Many of the students with disabilities who come into schoolwide investigations still come straight from substantially separate classrooms. Not only do they need to learn the Schools for Thought approach to investigations along with all the other entering students, but they need to learn how to work within a regular classroom setting. Lana Colburn, a district special education staff member who regularly visits the school, observes that students with disabilities need a full semester in the school to learn how to negotiate a heterogeneous classroom.

One of the continuing challenges is finding and retaining enough special education teachers, a problem for the whole district. It is not that there are fewer teachers being certified, but that St. Ellen teachers are drawn to teaching in the more affluent St. Ellen County Special School District, which serves many of the county's students with disabilities in a "virtual" district.

While special education teachers in the special school district receive the same beginning salaries as those in the St. Ellen district, their increments are considerably higher; so they have an incentive to teach for several years in the city schools and then move into the county (Morocco, Walker, & Lewis, 2003).

Sustaining Strong Leadership

District leaders in St. Ellen view Williams's leadership as critical to the school's success and to its inclusive approach for students with disabilities. They credit her leadership for sustaining a coherent, thinking model of instruction throughout the school (Morocco, Walker, & Lewis, 2003). They point to several characteristics of her leadership.

- *Sustained service in the school.* While the average length of service for current St. Ellen principals is under 5 years, the principal of Carter-Dean has been present since its founding, and many of the core faculty also have been present since then.
- *Use of assessment data to develop programs and partnerships.* The Carter-Dean principal is viewed by district leaders as adept at using research data to back up what she is asking for. In the words of Lisa Cox, "Williams can show agencies in the community her numbers."
- *Active response to change.* The principal's response to statewide testing pressures, involving her staff in understanding the problem and coming up with the best solution, including designing new curriculum materials, is typical of her active and highly collaborative response to changes from outside the school. One of the Carter-Dean feeder schools has a class of children with autism whose parents expect the group to move into Carter-Dean. Williams's response was, "Sure. Fine. What do we need to do to make them a part of the school in the fall?" District leaders see this as an example of her willingness to take on new challenges within the Schools for Thought structure and philosophy and to do whatever it takes to be successful.
- *Sharing leadership.* While the principal is clearly "first," teachers as a whole are decision makers. Faculty teams at each grade level are in charge of designing and revising curricula and setting policies that they think will benefit their students.

Sustaining the school through new times of reform and high-stakes testing will require that these important qualities continue in the school leader and faculty.

5

Signature Practices: Characteristics, Genesis, and Implications

This book contains detailed portraits of three schools, each of which has a unique signature practice. While each is distinct, all of these signature practices serve a common purpose. They help the schools to serve all of their students, including those who are particularly vulnerable because of disabilities and/or risks associated with poverty. Looking across the three schools, this chapter describes the major characteristics of the signature practices that contribute to their positive impact on students. It also explores what it takes to develop such a practice. A set of forces were at work in all three school communities that generated a signature practice that was right for each particular context. Finally, the chapter discusses the implications of the concept of schoolwide signature practice for the present federal and state reform milieu.

CHARACTERISTICS OF SCHOOLWIDE SIGNATURE PRACTICES

Across the schools we researched, the signature practices have three characteristics that contributed to their impact on students' learning. All of the practices have the following qualities:

- *Embedded*. The signature practice is grounded in a structure that makes it schoolwide.
- *Customized*. The signature practice is responsive to the cultures, strengths, and needs of the school's student population and to the social needs of the community.
- *Collaborative*. The signature practice creates and sustains a teacher learning community.

The Signature Practice Is Embedded in a Schoolwide Structure

What makes these schools unique is that their practices are situated within teaching and organizational structures that are by definition schoolwide. Each signature practice takes place within a larger structure that engages all faculty and content areas, and focuses the activity and resources of the school. The larger structures, although different across schools, have exactly the same relationship to the signature practice in every case. Interdisciplinary teaming is to co-teaching at Dolphin what the technology infrastructure is to exhibitions at Da Vinci and what interdisciplinary curriculum design by grade level is to investigations at Carter-Dean. That is, the larger organizational or curriculum structure supports the signature practice, helps to ensure its sustainability, and makes it schoolwide. It is unlikely the signature practice can survive as a schoolwide phenomenon over time without the organizational structure. Figure 5.1 portrays the relationships between each signature practice and its surrounding school structure.

This schoolwide structure supports and constrains what teachers can do. Carter-Dean teachers can assemble a rich range of resources for investigations because all the teachers at a grade level, along with the Science Center partnership, are focused on that unit. Teachers are expected to engage in Schools for Thought teaching and may be encouraged to transfer out if they do not own and participate in the approach. Every aspect of the school's leadership, selection of materials, and connections with the community coalesce around making the signature practice work, because it expresses the school's imperative for social equity and learning, and puts the imperative into action in a predictable way.

The result is *coherence* in how the school is organized to help every child learn. That coherence is a dynamic and ongoing process of design and modification within an established core structure. The Beacon schools integrated practices that expanded and strengthened their core vision, in contrast to what Dufour (2001) calls the "Christmas tree" approach to education reform in which

> Programs, training, and initiatives are simply hung on the existing structure and culture of the school like the ornaments of a Christmas tree [where] they dangle fragilely without ever being absorbed into the school's culture. (p. 16)

In a recent analysis of what it means for a school to have coherence, Honig and Hatch (2004) argue that in a coherent school, teachers and leaders are always crafting their specific goals and strategies (we would say

Figure 5.1. Benefits of a Customized Signature Practice in Three Schools

School and population	*Signature practice*	*Provides students*	*Allows all students to succeed*
Da Vinci Middle School, with a large number of Latino second-language learners	Exhibitions embedded in a schoolwide technology infrastructure	Technology tools for oral presentations in English or Spanish	By acquiring and demonstrating knowledge apart from language proficiency
Dolphin Middle School, with a large number of students with disabilities, linguistically varied immigrant students, and migrant students	Co-teaching embedded in schoolwide interdisciplinary teams	Two certified teachers using multiple approaches to teaching and learning	By benefiting from special education strategies to learn at their own pace
Carter-Dean Middle School, with both affluent White students and low-income Black students	Investigations embedded in grade-level interdisciplinary curricula with a science museum partner	Opportunities to collaborate in pursuit of a common body of knowledge	Through the opportunity for parity regardless of the knowledge-base with which they came to school

"practices") and engaging members of the community in that process. Da Vinci does this by regularly designing new exhibitions that measure students' learning and periodically engaging the community as audience and participant. Carter-Dean teachers craft and revise curriculum units with each incoming cohort of students and link the city's museums, particularly the Science Center, and other community resources to student investigations within those units.

The schools have a consistent stance from which to respond to external demands because the signature practice belongs to the whole school and reflects the beliefs that ground the school. In fact, Honig and Hatch (2004) argue that coherent schools actually "use external demands to advance their goals and strategies" (p. 19) rather than being thrown off course by those demands. The signature practice is the school's source of strength for responding to or pushing back on pressures from the outside. Da Vinci was required by the state to choose a school reform partner by the turn of the millennium, and the state assigned a "default" partner that did not fit the school's philosophy. The school then came up with its own choice— the Coalition of Essential Schools—which was congruent with its ideas about teaching and learning.

The embedded signature practice provides what Honig and Hatch (2004) call a "simplification system" for the school, a clear and relatively simple way to make decisions about what is best for its students and how it will respond to outside pressures. It provides the school a clear identity and confidence when leaders need to bargain for what is best for its students. Co-teaching within interdisciplinary teaming at Dolphin provides a forum for teachers, parents, students, and school leaders to talk through the effectiveness of their academic supports and family and student services. Coherence is thus "a social construction produced through continual interaction among teachers, students, organizational structures, curriculum, and other tools of schooling" (Honig & Hatch, 2004, p. 18). Embedded in meaningful schoolwide structures (see Figure 5.1), the signature practice is a way for each school to continually reinvent learning opportunities that fit its moral imperative and academic aspirations for all of its students.

The Signature Practice Is Customized

An equally important and related characteristic of the signature practice is that it is designed to serve the particular local student population in the school. In each case, the signature practice responds to and works to surmount a potential barrier to learning or treats it as a strength. As an example, many Da Vinci students (including students with disabilities) are just developing their English proficiency. Exhibitions respond to this potential barrier by emphasizing the value of communicating orally in English. Most second-language learners find that they can speak and understand spoken English more quickly than they can read or write it. The opportunity to represent their learning orally, with the assistance of visual technology tools, thus draws on and emphasizes students' strengths. While transitioning to English, second-language learners can engage in learning and expressing their knowledge of complex content.

Similarly, Dolphin students, many of whom have disabilities, are recent immigrants, and/or move in and out of the community with the changing seasons, benefit from a signature practice that provides additional, personalized teacher support. The practice assumes that varied learning styles are strengths to build upon. Carter-Dean students, who represent two groups from two different ethnic and socioeconomic backgrounds, benefit from cooperative investigations that provide a level playing field for developing investigative skills and deep content understanding. Cooperative investigations build on the opportunity for students with different backgrounds to learn and talk about truths about their society together.

Each school customized its signature practice and supporting organizational structure to build on and draw on the strengths of students' backgrounds, cultures, and linguistic variation. Figure 5.1 summarizes some ways in which the signature practice is customized in each school to students' backgrounds, strengths, and needs.

The Signature Practice Creates and Sustains a Professional Learning Community

All three signature practices, together with the structures that surround them, reflect highly collaborative approaches to teaching and learning. They involve teachers in working together on the intellectual tasks of planning, considering students' needs, designing curricula, teaching, and assessing results. At each grade level, Dolphin teachers work together in interdisciplinary teams to plan curricula, discuss students' progress, and coordinate very specific ways of supporting individual students through co-teaching. Carter-Dean teachers identify the topics and questions students will investigate and coordinate their content-area teaching around a set of shared big ideas, dilemmas, anchors, and consequential tasks. Da Vinci teachers plan and evaluate exhibitions and help one another's students refine their presentations. These activities reflect the kinds of teacher collaboration that, according to research on schools, builds professional communities and results in higher student achievement.

A key factor in professional learning communities is that teachers share a sense of responsibility for all students' learning, not simply those students in their own classrooms. That sense of joint responsibility correlates highly with student achievement (Louis, Kruse, & Marks, 1996). Professional learning in the schools we studied is directly related to the schools' beliefs and is "glued" to the goals of the signature practice. For example, Dolphin teams get help in teaching to multiple intelligences, while the Carter-Dean principal provides teachers with strategies for observing and coaching one another to deepen the conversations about students' investigations. Da Vinci teachers get help with new technology tools and strategies for teaching second-language learners.

Further, the signature practice provides a focus for teachers' joint planning and reflection. Teachers have a consistent language, various protocols, and common ways of doing things, which means they do not have to reinvent a way to approach each unit or lesson. Yet the signature practice is sufficiently open-ended that teachers frequently update the content and actively design their instruction together. There is room to agree or disagree as teachers decide what materials to use, what ideas are most important, and what skills are best aligned with statewide assessments. In fact, being able to disagree and air conflicts within an overall context of trust and shared goals makes for a strong school (Bryk & Schneider, 2002). A quality of the simplification system that we described above is that it has just this balance of specificity and openness (Newmann & Associates, 1996; Newmann & Wehlage, 1995).

The signature practices give teachers "decision frames"—frameworks in which to construct solutions and solve problems related to their students' learning and needs (Lave, 1991). The more teachers coalesce around an approach, some argue, the better they can make sense of the many varied messages about instruction that they may get from their districts, states, and professional associations (Coburn, 2001). The persistence of Carter-Dean's Schools for Thought unit format over 10 years reflects its usefulness in designing new curriculum units and updating existing ones.

One feature of a strong professional learning community is that it provides a structured way to initiate new teachers into the school (Lave, 1991; Palincsar, Magnusson, Marano, Ford, & Brown, 1998). The signature practice and the collaborative structure that surrounds it provide a clear set of criteria for the schools to use in bringing on new staff and helping them get acclimated to the school. Each school assigns mentors to new teachers, who learn by doing. Schools can, and these schools do, provide forms of apprenticeships for new teachers that acculturate them into very specific roles and rituals. For instance, new Carter-Dean teachers learn to cross talk, Da Vinci teachers master PowerPoint, and Dolphin teachers learn co-teaching—along with the beliefs, assumptions, and other features of the signature practice that support learning in each school.

WHAT IT TAKES TO CREATE A SIGNATURE PRACTICE

Different as the signature practices and student populations are in these schools, a set of commonalties underlie the development of these signature practices. Three creative forces interacted to generate a signature practice and a schoolwide organizational structure that works for each school. Figure 5.2 portrays the three forces that interacted in the genesis of each schoolwide signature practice. First, each school is the result of a moral imperative that extended from the principal to the school and the district,

Figure 5.2. The Genesis of a Signature Practice

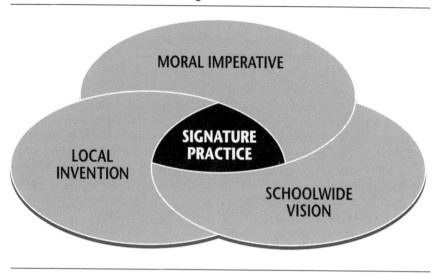

and connected with some national professional community that shared that imperative. Second, all three schools acted on a vision of an excellent middle school. Third, the schools participated in a process of local invention that brought varied stakeholders together.

Moral Imperative

The leaders of the three schools were driven by a sense of urgency to redress the inequalities of poverty, language, and special needs in their own communities. A moral imperative provided their rationale, or the *why* behind the creation of the signature practice. Each of the school leaders was an example of Fullan's (2003) argument that

> Moral purpose of the highest order is having a system where all students learn, the gap between high and low performance becomes greatly reduced, and what people learn enables them to be successful citizens and workers in a morally based knowledge society. (p. 29)

The principal at Carter-Dean said, "We *refuse* to believe that the connection between poverty and academic failure is a cycle that cannot be broken. We believe that students will achieve up to a school's expectations and we have continued to verbalize, require, and demonstrate examples of our expectations." The curriculum director at Da Vinci told the research team that "people don't expect high achievement from low-income students. But if you give them the skills, they *can* excel in mainstream society."

This sense of righteous indignation and a keen sense of the injustices of society drove these school leaders to find an approach to teaching that would level the playing field. Their mission was to provide students at risk for school failure and marginalized by society with access to a rigorous curriculum and a place in our competitive society.

The school leaders did not hold a moral imperative only as individuals, however. They extended it to faculty, parents, and even students within the school by "establishing a climate of relationship trust" (Fullan, 2003, p. 65) within which the staff could openly and honestly tackle tough issues. The leaders extended the imperative throughout the school by bringing together faculty who shared the imperative and by building trusting relationships with other staff that emphasized respect, personal regard for others, competence, and integrity (Bryk & Schneider, 2002).

The principals each used the relational trust they built to ensure universal buy-in of teachers for the signature practice. Occasionally, this entailed tough love—as at Dolphin, where the assistant principal reported, "We told the teachers they would be co-teaching. Then we locked them in a room together and said, 'Don't come out until you can tell us how you're going to do it.'" Not only teachers but also students had to buy into the signature practice. By the time our research team identified the schools, the teachers, administrators, and students alike shared a sense of urgency about the school's mission to right the injustices that left students vulnerable in the larger social and education system.

Where the schools may differ, however, is in the extent to which their sense of moral imperative was as passionately shared by their central office district staff. In Da Vinci and Carter-Dean, the school–district connection was strong, particularly during the founding of the schools. In contrast, Dolphin's district assumed a more passive role. While they accepted the need for a redesigned middle school, district staff did not become deeply involved in its founding. However, district leaders may have been grateful that the Dolphin leaders and faculty were devoted to the most needy student population in the district.

Schoolwide Instructional Vision

If the moral imperative provides the *why* of transforming the schools, each school's vision provides *what* the transformation should look like. These schools are three among many that struggled to transform themselves from traditional junior high schools to a new idea of a middle school. They were more successful than most because they drew on important national ideas and then developed practices that suited their own needs within the middle school framework. They matched their response to local needs with compelling ideas about teaching, learning, and middle-grades reform. The core beliefs outlined in each of the cases hold the images of what is important and what learning might look like in the school. In each case, those core beliefs and the school's signature practice as it finally was crafted resonate with the big ideas of the middle school movement.

- The signature practices are developmentally responsive in building on young adolescents' capacity for abstract thinking and their need for connections to one another and to adults.
- They promote academic excellence by engaging all students in researching and investigating important questions.
- They embrace social equity by allowing all students to demonstrate their competence, regardless of social class, facility of language, and special needs.

In rooting the signature practice in a strong vision for the school, the Beacon schools behaved like charter schools. A study of innovation in Massachusetts charter schools found that charter schools (excluding the for-profits) tend to be based on a vision or mission, which leads to the coherent and integrated adoption of instructional practices that cluster around the vision. This is in contrast with other public schools, which tend to adopt instructional practices additively, without a systematic focus (Brigham & Rosenblum, 1998).

Collaborative Local Invention

Through local invention, the school founders decided *how* they would realize their vision. Several characteristics of the local innovation process in the three schools appeared to be critical to birthing the signature practices and nurturing and supporting them in schoolwide structures that created ownership and coherence across the school. These characteristics included a mandate from the district coupled with time for exploration and design, participation by partners and organizations beyond the schools and district, and a central district office as a provider of support to schools.

A mandate coupled with exploration. First, each school had an urgent mandate from the district, coupled with time for exploration and design, a condition that rarely exists for changing schools. The mandate came from conditions or crises from within and beyond the district. In all three schools, overcrowding caused the districts to set in motion the design of a new school; at Da Vinci and Carter-Dean that overcrowding was happening particularly at the middle school level. And in two of the districts, a larger crisis shaped the direction that school design would take. At Da Vinci, the threat of state takeover of very low-performing districts precipitated a complete change in leadership and a paradigm shift in how the district as a whole thought about education for a student population that was overwhelmingly low-income and Latino. At Carter-Dean, the crisis was court-ordered desegregation in a city still holding onto segregated schools and segregationist policies. That court order also included the stipulation that at least 30 students with disabilities be admitted to every magnet school.

Within this urgent requirement for change, the founding principals, teachers, and district staff had a window of opportunity to broaden their knowledge and thinking. The local innovation process included opportunities for school and district staff to engage in studying reform practices, visiting other schools, and linking with research on learning as well as the researchers themselves. "We read about what was going on in middle-grades reforms. We saw that staying with kids for at least 2 years helps teachers respond to kids' learning needs," the Dolphin principal said. The Carter-Dean founders made four different visits to schools in New York, California, and Tennessee to inform themselves about instruction that helps young adolescents use their thinking abilities.

The pressure for change was intense, yet all three schools and districts captured space for reflection and a deliberative design process. Within a relatively relaxed time frame provided by the districts, founders engaged in study and discussion—but also experienced the chaos and confusion that are often critical for transforming individuals and institutions. Yet they supported one another and got sufficient support from the districts to use this period constructively to invent practices and structures around ideas they cared about.

Collaborations beyond the schools and districts. Further, the process took place over months and years, involving some consultants and organizations from beyond the districts. The Dolphin co-teaching model was a dynamic concept that changed as teachers learned more about the practice from research on co-teaching and middle schools. The principal began a connection with the National Middle School Association that resulted, some years later, in his taking on the presidency of the organization.

Carter-Dean piloted investigative learning practices in an existing middle school over a 2-year period. And the Carter-Dean staff interacted with cognitive scientists in several parts of the country before pulling their model of investigations together in a new building. Da Vinci worked with a private-sector organization, Bell Atlantic, in one of the more innovative experiments in technology—placing computers in the homes of low-income Latino students and wiring the school for use of the exploding Internet technology. Da Vinci also used interactions with the Coalition and with consultants from Education Development Center's Center for Children and Technology in New York City to think through the role of technology in inquiry learning.

The school founders used these connections to inform and shape their own thinking. They limited the interactions to what they needed and incorporated new ideas into their emerging models. They clarified previously elusive goals and strategies to reflect new knowledge that they got from wider reform groups (Elmore, 1996; McLaughlin & Talbert, 2001).

District office as a support provider. In each of the school cases, the district and school were, in various ways, partners in the designing of a new school. This is a departure from the traditional hierarchical view that schools execute policies set out by the district (Honig, 2004). It is also different from charter schools, where the district very much limits its role in school development. The process in these three schools was neither a top-down mandate from the district as to how the schools should respond to the local crisis, nor a complete bottom-up process that would give the school exclusive control over the design process.

Instead, the schools and districts engaged in a mutual process of goal setting and negotiation that contributed to the schools' emerging goals and practices. While a detailed story of the interactions between the school and central office in each case is beyond the scope of this book, we did find evidence that the districts, for the most part, played a support role rather than a directive one in advancing the schools' *own* goals and decision-making processes.

In some cases more than others, district staff also helped buffer and manage outside pressures on the school (Honig & Hatch, 2004). This was particularly the case for Da Vinci and Carter-Dean. Da Vinci served as a *laboratory* within the district for designing new approaches to teaching and learning. The approaches reflected a vision of active, computer-supported learning for low-income, second-language learners that persists throughout the district today. As the middle school grew, the district supported and learned from it, and helped to diffuse successful practices out to other middle schools and up into the high schools. At Carter-Dean, particularly during the founding stage, the district provided *protective support* so that the school could design a model that fulfilled court orders for a racially balanced school and provided for the inclusion of students with disabilities in a magnet school. The school provided resources for travel, and special education experts in the district kept protective watch over the school in its first years.

Honig and Hatch (2004) characterize this relationship between school and district as "crafted coherence," an "ongoing process whereby schools and district central offices work together to help schools manage external demands" (p. 26). The authors define three activities that crafted coherence entails.

> (a) Schools establish their own goals and strategies. These goals and strategies typically are specific and open-ended, as well as adaptable, and developed through sustained and managed school-based participatory activities. (b) Schools use their goals and strategies as the basis for deciding whether to bridge or buffer external demands. (c) District central offices support these decision-making processes by continually searching for and using information about school goals, strategies, and experiences to inform their own operations. (p. 26)

A district may achieve its own goals through serving the school's needs, taking on the role of a "buffer" against outside pressures and a "bridge" to outside resources (Honig & Hatch, 2004). This process is not a straightforward one; school designers need opportunities for trail and error—a "muddling through" rather than a clear pathway (Behn, 1988; Kanter, 1988).

Of the three cases, the United City School District best exemplifies crafted coherence in the way it closely observed and supported Leonardo da Vinci's pioneering technology efforts. In doing so, the district staff learned how schools can organize around exhibitions and used that learning to plan how the districts' high schools could engage their students in using computers as tools for investigating important topics and communicating their information and ideas within and beyond the school.

In contrast, the district staff in Miner County was more passive in their support for Dolphin than the other two districts with regard to not only the moral imperative but also the actual school design process. They provided support in the form of time for exploration, but largely left the principal, assistant principal, and founding teachers on their own to develop the school's design. Dolphin's success with the lowest income students— many of them children of migrant workers and new immigrant parents— was critical to the health of the larger community. At the same time, the school's "champions" and ardent participants in the design process were largely within the school.

While this kind of autonomy and permission may seem an advantage for the school, particularly with leaders who have strong ideas and great energy for change as the Dolphin leaders did, there are disadvantages. As external pressures for statewide achievement ratcheted up, Dolphin required inventive support from the district to keep the school's signature practice and approach to inclusion intact. However, district attention was focusing on the lowest performing students in statewide tests. The state mandated that districts provide intensive reading and mathematics instruction outside the classroom to those students, many of whom included students with disabilities. District special education leaders continued to believe fully in providing students with disabilities support in the general education classroom. In fact, Miner County currently (in 2005) has over 63% of its students with disabilities served in general education classes for 80% or more of their school day, the third highest in the state of Florida. Nevertheless, the attention and resources needed to sustain the presence of a special education teacher in each team—who would "train" the content teachers and co-teach within the general education classroom—diminished in the school by 2001.

Substantially separate classrooms and curricula increased, and a separation between content teachers and special education teachers grew and widened. Furthermore, the school leadership changed and founding teachers decided that their signature practice was no longer right for students. In Chapter 1, it was a Dolphin assistant principal who gave up on the school's vision and signature practice, and declared with considerable pain, "Everything we've been doing is wrong." In the Dolphin school community, where local innovation was more permissive the signature practice had a robust life for close to 10 years, and then faded in the life of the school.

In contrast, in the two other cases, where the districts were more intensely involved in the founding and in the continuing protection and support of the school, the signature practices have been sustained. They remain intact and vital at the end of the 2005 school year, although there is a difference between these two schools in the kind of support they now receive from the district. The principal of Carter-Dean remains "on the edge" as the larger district contemplates "leveling" the entire district around one form of education—direct instruction. This would signal the end of investigative learning in one of the very highest performing schools in the district, with both general and special education students.

In contrast, the Da Vinci community continues to see the school as an exemplar of a kind of learning that the district cares about and believes in. The new principal at Da Vinci has opened a new building that has enabled Da Vinci to spread out and accommodate up to 600 students, all within an exhibitions approach to teaching and learning. Exhibitions continue to occur at the end of each marking period, and students use an expanded set of technology tools to conduct their research and present their learning to the school and to the community. The district provides a cart in each classroom that is wired to the Internet, networked to the all of the students' computers, includes a CD-ROM and VHS player, and can project any material on walls that are kept painted bright white for that purpose. The assistant principal experiences enduring support from central office staff, who continue to protect this high-performing school from intensive state achievement pressure as the school's eighth graders continue to perform at the top of the district on statewide tests.

During a recent visit to the newly opened building, a member of the research team, somewhat lost in the school's new neighborhood, encountered a Latina mother of a Da Vinci graduate. The parent walked the visitor to the school. The parent said she had just received an invitation to the upcoming Expo, even though her daughter is now in college. "We all go," she laughed as she ushered the visitor into a wide lobby with banners in Spanish and English.

LESSONS OF LOCAL INVENTION IN AN ERA
OF FEDERAL AND STATE REFORM

A school cannot go out and buy or borrow a signature practice, and a district cannot mandate one. It must result from the school's commitment to academic excellence, social equity, and developmental responsiveness for its own population. If a school wishes to develop a signature practice, however, the three schools we studied offer several lessons.

One lesson is that an instructional practice intended to level the playing field for students who are challenged by disability, poverty, and/or English language status can result in a school that is academically excellent for *all* students. One might think that a school's success in serving students with disabilities as well as typical students might be simply a by-product rather than a deliberate focus of reform, much like the notion that a rising tide raises all boats.

Instead, we found schools in which the success of students with disabilities was *integral* to the school's definition of success and the school's design for achieving that success. Students with disabilities may be the most vulnerable students in urban schools because they often face risks associated with both poverty and disabilities. Da Vinci, Dolphin, and Carter-Dean believed that by taking into account their most vulnerable students in designing their schools, they could find solutions that would be effective for most students.

The essential question that drives the development of a signature practice is, "What instructional tool will give the *students in this school* optimum access to the curriculum and opportunities to increase and demonstrate their academic skills and understanding?"

A second lesson is that developing a signature practice also requires a whole-school commitment, beginning with but not confined to the school's leaders. Also, based on our research, the practice can be sustained only when it is embedded in a schoolwide structure that enables it to work for all students and teachers. That structure may draw on research-based practices and approaches taking place far from the school—so the whole school's involvement in surveying current practice and research can expand and clarify the planners' thinking.

Finally, although a school's vision and goals need to drive the process of innovation, the district's engagement, resources, and ongoing negotiation and support are critical to the longevity of the signature practice. The experiences of these three schools suggest that schools require time to reflect on their strengths and problems, pursue and explore alternatives, gather information from research and broader reform communities, and invent or choose practices that work best, given local needs and conditions.

The schools in this study developed during the time in which the middle school movement blossomed, whole-school reform was highly touted in education, and inclusion was the watchword of the disabilities community. The schools were—and, in two cases, continue to be—so advanced in each of these areas that we might expect them to be viewed nationally and in their states and districts as the cutting edge of reform. But that is not the case. In the 5 years since we completed the Beacons of Excellence study, the pendulum has reversed drastically, driven by the power of federal mandates.

The federal government has a history of issuing mandates that affect education. The most important of these have been attempts to level the playing field for vulnerable populations. Title I addresses the needs of students in economically disadvantaged schools; desegregation legislation focuses on the rights of minorities; and IDEA addresses the rights of people with disabilities. Each of these has behind it the force of a moral imperative. No Child Left Behind (NCLB) also uses the language of moral force, but it represents a *political* shift by the federal government. It is an intervention that specifies outcomes for all students as well as the measures by which those outcomes will be judged, and does not focus on the teaching and learning that can contribute to those outcomes. It tends to ignore the topography of the playing field and focus mainly on the score. We have argued that these inventive schools were shaped by three creative forces: a moral imperative, an instructional vision, and local innovation. It is unlikely that these forces will be encouraged to come together in this era of NCLB. Figure 5.3 contrasts the driving concerns of the Beacons schools with those of NCLB.

Schools are poised at the crossroads of change once again. NCLB has been in effect for several years, and principals, teachers, and students are now immersed in state standards and assessments. The jury is still out on

Figure 5.3. Driving Concerns in Beacons Schools versus NCLB

Concerns driving the Beacons schools	Concerns of NCLB
Internal to the school and community	External
A moral imperative based on social justice	A political imperative to fix the system
A focus on teaching and learning	A focus on outcomes
A high value placed on local innovation	Little or no value placed on local innovation
Intention to bridge the achievement gap	Measurement of the achievement gap

the impact of NCLB on student learning. Many applaud the legislation for making schools accountable for their students' performance on statewide reading and math assessments. Others are not so sure. A report by Education Trust, *Stalled in Secondary: A Look at Student Achievement Since the No Child Left Behind Act* (2005), focuses on student performance in 27 states and reports that many states are not making progress in closing achievement gaps. Twenty-four states improved overall performance in math; in reading, only 16 improved. Reading achievement declined in eight states and did not change in three. "In reading at the middle grades, more states saw achievement gaps narrow than grow wider. But in some cases, those gaps narrowed because the achievement of white students went down" (p. 2). In math, the Latino–White gap "grew wider or stayed the same in more states than it narrowed. And the gap between poor and non-poor students grew or remained the same in nine states. In only three states did the income gap narrow" (p. 2).

The Rand Report, *Achieving State and National Literacy Goals, A Long Uphill Road: A Report to the Carnegie Corporation of New York* (McCombs et al., 2004), examines results of state reading tests and the National Assessment of Educational Progress reading assessment for each of the 50 states and finds that both show large achievement gaps between subgroups of students, disaggregated by race/ethnicity and poverty status. Further, at both fourth- and eighth-grade levels, students with limited English proficiency and students with disabilities trail well behind their peers. The report concludes that the "wide disparity in the achievement of subgroups of students makes reaching the 100-percent-proficiency goal even more difficult, particularly for states, districts, and schools with large proportions of such subgroups" (p. 61).

The national focus is now shifting to high school, where dropout rates, poor attendance, and low scores in math and reading cry out for attention. Organizations focusing on high schools are leading the charge in calling for change. The 2005 National Education Summit on High Schools "sought to redefine the role of the high school in America while better connecting its curriculum to the expectations that high school graduates will face in college and the workforce," and developed "a five-point action agenda states can follow to raise graduation rates and close preparation gaps" (Alliance for Excellent Education, 2005b, p. 1). The *NASSP Legislative Recommendations for High School Reform* (National Association of Secondary School Principals, 2005) states that "the historical structures and purpose of the U.S. high school are no longer adequate to serve the needs of all of the nation's youth and provide them with the skills necessary to compete in the global marketplace of the twenty-first century," and recommends eight areas for reform (p. 2).

As was the case with middle schools in the 1990s, foundations, schools, reform organizations, and passionate school leaders are working together to respond to a crisis in education and to reinvent schools—this time high schools. Energetic reforms that include smaller learning communities, high school academies, freshman "ramp up" programs, and expanded numbers of charter schools signal a time of local invention, particularly in city schools. Although President Bush is urging that funds be directed to high schools (Alliance for Excellent Education, 2005a), the funds are to be directed to support assessment plans, with much less support for the improvement of school designs and the quality of teaching and learning that is the foundation for higher achievement. As No Child Left Behind extends high-stakes testing into the high school, the critical questions are, Will local innovations thrive or be stifled? Can high school reform learn from the middle-grades reform movement ways to balance external pressures with local invention?

The biggest lesson from Da Vinci, Dolphin, and Carter-Dean is that the most equitable solutions for schools come from freedom to innovate around the particular needs and cultures of students. If schools are to generate schoolwide signature practices that respond to the strengths, cultures, and needs of their students, they will require support, services, and collaboration from their communities and districts. They will require federal and state policies that recognize the power of informed local invention and decision making in building academically excellent and equitable schools for all of our youth.

Epilogue

In these case studies we see the power of local invention, as the principals, teachers, parents, students, and reform partners in three schools craft a vision and a way of learning that includes all groups of students. What message for the 21st century can we take from these vibrant schools of the 1990s? One could argue that these schools were successful because they mobilized locally responsive programs just *before* the No Child Left Behind engine fully took hold; they had time and the resources to develop and demonstrate their signature practices. Are these schools in the vanguard of reform or are they irrelevant in a climate of high-stakes tests and federal mandates?

We would argue that these schools are timely exemplars of how reforms that respond to local needs and opportunities can succeed in a time of federal mandates. The schools faced pressures other than emerging high-stakes testing and NCLB demands. One school was threatened with a federal court takeover, a second faced possible state takeover, and all three faced demands from their districts that they solve the problem of overcrowding. In each case, the schools managed multiple pressures and negotiated perilous decisions about school structure, staffing, and philosophy. At a time when statewide tests were narrowing the mission of schooling, the adults in these reforming communities saw—like many educators and parents today—a need to engage students' minds in inquiry. They didn't flinch from teaching approaches that lead students to ask questions, gather information, and form independent judgments about difficult issues.

Our current middle and high schools have some support for local innovation from state and national leaders. In recent hearings on NCLB, a number of governors and legislators argued that the federal government needs to "go slow" in instituting more testing requirements at the high school level. They argued for time and incentives for schools to innovate and bring varied solutions to the table. The current Striving Readers initiative is providing funds for a coalition of middle and high schools and reform organizations to implement and study varied approaches to improving literacy in lower-income schools. These funded projects are likely to bring a variety of local visions and solutions to discussions of what secondary schools should look like.

As authors, our moral imperative was to tell the stories of these schools to current school leaders. Inspired by what the schools teach about successful innovation, current leaders can engage their staff and community members in articulating their beliefs about what is morally *good*. Fired by that passion, schools can look beyond mandates to the heart of accountability—shared responsibility for educating students who understand how to mobilize human ingenuity and solve challenges beyond our current imagining.

How We Found and Studied the Schools

In order to identify the visionary schools that were to become the focus of our study, we sought urban middle schools that were working toward goals of developmental responsiveness, academic excellence, and social equity. We sought schools that, as part of their mission of social equity, intentionally set out to serve all of their students, including those with identified disabilities, those acquiring English proficiency, and those recently immigrated to the United States. We considered only schools with strong records of progress on various measures of academic learning, including statewide standards-based tests. Once we identified the schools, we used a combination of qualitative and quantitative approaches to learn how they worked and why they were successful with diverse groups of students, including those with disabilities. Over the next 2 years, with the help of the schools themselves, we unearthed what made them "beacons" and what they could teach us about local solutions to the crises of middle-grades education.

This appendix details the methods we used to throughout the five steps of our research:

1. refining the research questions,
2. identifying the schools and establishing trust,
3. collecting data,
4. analyzing data, and
5. integrating data across schools.

REFINING THE RESEARCH QUESTIONS

The middle-grades tripod provided the framework for our initial research questions (see Figure A.1). In addition, we posed questions about how students experienced the schools, roles and challenges for school leaders, and

Figure A.1. Research Questions

Developmental Responsiveness. What is the evidence that all groups of students have a sense of safety and belonging? How is learning personalized for students? How is learning structured to capitalize on the intellectual strengths of young adolescents?

Academic Excellence. How well do all groups of students in the school achieve on district and statewide tests? How rigorous is the learning in connecting with standards, important content, and content relevant to students' lives and futures beyond school? What other evidence can the school provide for academic excellence?

Social Equity. Who is important in the school? What groups have access to academic challenges and opportunities for social connection? What groups have leadership opportunities?

Student Experience of the School. How do students with varying kinds of disabilities and varying cultural backgrounds experience the academic curriculum, academic support, and daily life in school?

School Leadership. What roles did principals play in the founding of the school? What role do they play in promoting an integrated vision and program?

District and Community Context. What contextual factors in and beyond the school contribute to developmental responsiveness, academic achievement, and social equity for students, including students with disabilities?

---

schools' and districts' history and policies that contributed to the schools' success. We expected that these questions would lead to others and that we eventually would elaborate the framework to reflect what we learned.

IDENTIFYING THE SCHOOLS AND ESTABLISHING TRUST

Colleagues well positioned within the middle-grades reform movement expected that while we would find urban middle-grades schools that were both responsive to young adolescents and academically high performing with at least some groups of students, we would be challenged to find schools that also were successfully including students with disabilities in general classroom learning. But over the course of a yearlong search, we were able to find several such schools.

We initially cast a wide net to catch as many schools as possible that met the following criteria:

- Demonstrated evidence of being attuned to the needs of all adolescent students
- Practiced a rigorous curriculum with high expectations for all students, including students with disabilities
- Included all students, including students with disabilities, in every facet of school life
- Demonstrated evidence of a 3-year trajectory of positive academic achievement

We sought nominations from National Middle-Grades Forum and Collaborative members, EDC's school networks, middle school experts, and national organizations. We invited schools to nominate themselves through a mailing to all Great City Schools and posted a call in journals and newsletters read by middle school principals. The final total was 59 nominated schools from all over the country, with many grade configurations, including grades 6–8 of K–8 schools.

We used a net of finer mesh for the application process. In addition to requesting 3 years of statistics about the school's academic performance, the application asked schools to write an essay on how they were academically excellent, developmentally responsive, and socially equitable. We counseled out schools that fit most criteria but did not yet integrate students with disabilities into regular classrooms and curricula. To select finalists for site visits, the research team developed scoring rubrics for each of the tripod dimensions, and two researchers read and scored each application and winnowed the applicant group to eight finalists. We were mindful of advice from our school administrator-advisors that to be credible, the final schools should look like other urban middle schools in this country—large, well established, and serving urban, culturally diverse populations.

At least two members of the research team visited each school, using the scoring rubric to summarize our observations. During the visit, we asked clarifying questions that had arisen when we discussed the applications and met with administrators, groups of teachers, parents and community members, and students. We observed in classrooms and talked with students in their gathering places. We collected additional quantitative data on academic results. Following the visits, we made a final selection, based on a combination of quantitative data, qualitative data, and the ratings on our rubrics. Although we left behind some very appealing schools with very positive academic and social trajectories, we were satisfied that the three Beacons schools met our criteria and were willing to work with us to unpack their success.

We conducted early and open negotiations about how to make the study an exchange of equivalent value for us and the schools. Early on, the principals revealed, each in his or her own way, why they chose to participate. We negotiated with each school during and even after the initial site selection process about what the project could mean to the school, what we would do for them, and what they would do for the study and the eventual readers of our reports. For example, the principal of Dolphin initially hoped that the partnership would help his school manage an upcoming district evaluation of the school. While we could not focus on his evaluation, we could share general observations and survey data that he could draw on in his reports. Williams, principal of Carter-Dean, saw the study as a "just in time" partner to alert the school faculty to issues related to very individual learning needs. The Leonardo Da Vinci principal asked for ongoing feedback, something that was painfully lacking in the school's previous encounters with outside groups. We agreed to provide a summary of the goals and results of each of our visits to the school within two weeks of the visit, as well to provide the school with the results of our school climate survey with teachers, students, and parents. These conversations laid a critical foundation of mutual understanding. Monitoring the schools' sense of the fairness of the investigation, having school and district leaders review reports and articles for accuracy, and strictly observing the schools' protocols for "guests of the house" all contributed to a respectful relationship that over time give us access to the schools' beliefs and practices.

COLLECTING DATA: A MIXED METHODS APPROACH

The questions we posed (see Figure A.1) required that we gather both qualitative data (observation, interview, student work, focus groups) and quantitative data (scores from district and state tests, surveys). This research approach is currently being called a "new wave" or "third paradigm" (Johnson & Onwuegbuzie, 2004) because it offers an alternative to the usual polarization of experimental and qualitative research (Guba & Lincoln, 1994). While all research in the social sciences attempts to provide supported assertions about human beings and the environments in which they live and evolve (Biesta & Burbules, 2003), traditional experiments are designed to *test* hypotheses, while qualitative studies discover patterns and may *generate* hypotheses. Mixed methods research brings together the perspectives, techniques, and language of these two paradigms into a single study in order to both discover patterns and also test and verify them (Frechtling & Sharp, 1997; Tashakkori & Teddlie, 1998).

The methods we used are described individually below. But the complexity of our research required that we frequently use multiple methods to study single events in order to gather several perspectives. For example, in conducting a classroom observation, we not only kept a running observation record, but also might interview one or more students and the teacher in the process, and collect student work from the same day.

The Surveys

The survey instruments that we used (see Appendix B) ask students, teachers, and parents for their viewpoint on students' sense of safety and belonging, the academic rigor of the school, parents' own sense of importance and belonging, and students' motivation to learn. The surveys had these additional features:

- They asked the same or similar questions of students, teachers, and families to assess the extent of agreement among stakeholder groups.
- Surveys were coded to identify students with disabilities in order to compare their responses with those of the general population.
- Surveys also were coded by grade level.
- Teacher surveys were coded to identify special education teachers.
- Parent surveys were translated into Spanish for Latino families.
- A teacher read the student survey aloud to ensure that those with language and reading difficulties were included.[1]

Achievement Data

Research staff collected district achievement data as a part of the application process and each year of the study, to document whether the schools were on a trajectory of academic excellence for both the general population and special education students. The results for the Beacons schools also were compared will those for the district as a whole or demographically similar schools in the district.

Interviews and Focus Groups

Research staff conducted formal and informal interviews with individuals and groups at several points over the course of the research. Interviews with parents in the mainly Latino school included one or more teachers who could translate for parents. Some of these interviews focused on a single key issue, such as the school's vision or philosophy concerning inclusion, and others covered a range of issues around instructional practice or curriculum development.

Classroom Observations

The research team observed instruction in over 100 classrooms and special education settings. After reviewing a number of observation protocols, the staff decided to use a nonstructured format to allow for maximum flexibility in the observation process. The observer kept a near-verbatim running record of the teachers' verbal and nonverbal interactions with students and as detailed a record of students' interactions as possible. Where we encountered co-teaching, two members of the study team observed—one focused on the general education teacher and students, while the other followed the special education teacher and students with disabilities.

Shadowing

In shadowing, an observer follows a child throughout the school day to observe and "participate" in classroom work, including formal and informal interactions with teachers and peers, through the lens of the child's experience.[2] While shadowing can be used to develop case studies of individual students, in our study it served to open windows onto the *schools*.

In each school, we chose (in consultation with administrators) students that represented various groups of learners (e.g., students with disabilities, typical students, at-risk students, second-language learners) in order to unearth how different kinds of students experience a day and what programs, practices, and structure propel their learning. Shadowing field notes across six or more classes brought to the surface recurring kinds of events and activities and provoked a rich set of questions about how the school worked for students with different kinds of needs and abilities. To provide a context for the snapshot offered by shadowing as well as avenues for exploring questions and interpretations, the observer also interviewed the student's parent(s), the teachers observed over the course of the day, and the student himself or herself.

ANALYZING THE DATA

Reliability and Validity

Teacher insights and sensitivity are valuable tools for the investigation. They also introduce bias and potentially slant interpretations in a particular direction. We used a number of strategies to manage bias and ensure that interpretations drew on several different sources of data, as well as several different research perspectives. We wanted to hold to the standard that quantitative research calls *internal validity* and qualitative research names *credibility*, the assurance that what we described or reported actually happened in the schools. Strategies for internal validity or credibility include being in the schools over an extended period of time, conducting many observations and debriefing every set of observations and interviews within our research team, "triangulating" data by comparing the results of one kind of data with the results of other kinds, and checking our interpretations with members of the school.

We were equally concerned about another standard—the relevance of our findings to other schools—which quantitative research refers to as *external validity* and qualitative research calls *transferability* (Anfara, Brown, & Mangione, 2002). We maximized external validity by selecting schools in different parts of the country with varied demographic characteristics, providing detailed ("thick") descriptions of what we saw, and purposefully sampling events within the school to include a wide range of subject areas, kinds of students, and kinds of challenges to the school (Anfara et al., 2002).

Finally, we were committed to data that is *reliable*, in quantitative research terms, or *dependable*, in qualitative research terms. By this we mean that the process of the study is consistent and reasonably stable over time and across researchers and methods—that things have been done carefully (Miles & Huberman, 1994). We documented all research activities, developed coding schemes over several iterations, compared the results of different data sources, and drew on the perspectives of all research team members in developing interpretations. Figure A.2. displays these standards and strategies.

Analysis Tasks

Our major analysis effort occurred once the surveys, site visits, interviews, and classroom observations were completed. At that point, the staff undertook a variety of tasks to (1) reduce and interpret the data, (2) create data displays, (3) interpret the findings through multiple iterations, and (4) integrate findings across schools.

Because there is less consensus around standards for reliability in naturalistic inquiry than for experimental research, we will describe how, through these steps, we arrived at the central finding of this work—that the three schools organized not only teaching and learning but the entire school around a central practice that reflected a coherent set of beliefs and an educational mission with the force of moral imperative.

Figure A.2. Strategies to Promote Validity and Reliability

Quantitative term	Qualitative term	Strategy used
Internal validity	Credibility	• Prolonged engagement in sites • Use of peer debriefing • Triangulation • Member checks
External validity	Transferability	• Provide thick descriptions • Purposive sampling • Select varied sites and populations
Reliability	Dependability	• Create a paper trail • Code and recode • Triangulation • Peer examination of interpretations

Source: Adapted from Anfara et al. (2002)

Reduce and interpret the data. First, each separate source of quantitative and qualitative data had to be organized and meaningfully reduced or reconfigured, not only for the sake of manageability, but to make the data intelligible in relation to the research questions (Miles & Huberman, 1994). From the surveys of teachers, regular and special education students, and families, the staff statistically clustered items that measured related variables. We were particularly interested in items or groups of items that reflected the school's responsiveness to adolescents' developmental needs for belonging ("I belong in this school," "I feel safe in this school"), peer collaboration ("Students work together"), support from adults ("Teachers give me the help I need"), and social equity ("when people pick on me, I think it is because of my race"). To analyze qualitative data, we first assembled all data sources within each school (focus groups, observations, interviews conducted with multiple parties) around each research question and then developed coding systems that could apply across data sources.

Create data displays. We used tables, charts, or matrices to compare the responses of stakeholder groups with one another in terms of items related to developmental responsiveness, academic excellence, and social equity. For example, the bar graph in Figure A.3 displays the viewpoints

Figure A.3. Survey Data Results

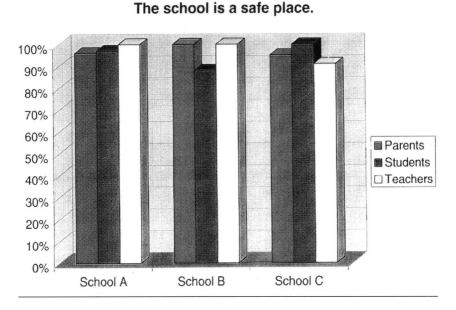

The school is a safe place.

of parents, students, and teachers by school for a survey item from the project that is directly related to developmental responsiveness, agreement with the statement, "The school is a safe place." In qualitative analysis, the data display goes a step beyond data reduction to provide an organized assembly of information that permits the research to draw conclusions (Miles & Huberman, 1994). Data displays can be extended text, diagrams, charts, or matrices that provide a new way of arranging or thinking about more textually embedded data.

Interpret the findings. The challenge of a study with many kinds of data is to make public the focus of each iteration and the steps by which the researcher arrived at findings. Figure A.4 provides a schema of three iterations of analysis that we carried out in the study, similar to other studies that include qualitative methods to generate hypotheses through induction (Anfara, Brown, & Mangione, 2002). The schema is illustrated with examples from Carter-Dean.

The first iteration reveals many different kinds of events, practices, and situations—emerging "codes" that ultimately may or may not prove to be directly relevant to the focus of the research and/or related to one another

Figure A.4. Iterative Data Analysis: Emergence of the Signature Practice

Data analysis	Result/finding	Carter-Dean example
First iteration: Look for recurrences	Many categories of activity in school	Cross talk, pods, rotations, questions, field trips, computer-based essays
Second iteration: Map patterns	Activities are parts of larger units	Cross talk, pods, rotations, questions, etc., are all features of investigations.
Third iteration: Triangulate data sources	Varied data sources show similar patterns and confirm their meaning to all participants	Investigations are the school's signature practice—a consistent and coherent approach to including all students in rigorous learning.

(Anfara et al., 2002). The goal is to examine what is there and label it (Patton, 2001).

The goal for the second iteration is the search for patterns that represent connections and relationships among the initial set of discrete categories. Entities identified in the first iteration may be members of a bigger category, part of a series, alternative approaches used for the same purpose, nested within one another, and so on.

As patterns emerge, they suggest, in the third iteration, hypotheses, explanations, or "theories" about what is important to participants and how things work in a setting. The researchers return to the data for confirmation—to see whether categories and patterns developed in the first two iterations are consistent with and fit the explanations. When a hypothesis or explanation is confirmed, it becomes a finding.

Integrating findings across schools. For each school, we documented recurrences, mapped patterns, and triangulated data sources around emerging findings. Because these within-school analyses were taking place concurrently across the three schools, we were aware of similarities and differences across the schools. In a more systematic set of comparisons, we found that while the schools initially looked similar by our initial middle-grades reform criteria and framework, they differed in *how* they created an equitable school and achieved academic success. Each school had particular ways of approaching the curriculum, organizing how people worked together, working with parents, and carrying out instruction in the classroom.

The key finding—which is developed and illustrated through the three case studies—was that each school developed a different schoolwide instructional practice related to its core beliefs. Every structural and organizational aspect of the school in some way contributed to or supported that way of learning. The practice was pervasive, involving almost all students and teachers throughout the school. Perhaps because they were so deeply embedded in the school's daily life and *culture*, it took us many visits and iterations of data analysis to see the signature practices sharply etched.

Student, Teacher, and Parent Surveys

STUDENT SURVEY

Tell Us About Yourself.

A1. Gender: Male ☐   Female ☐

A2. Race

                African American ☐
                Caucasian ☐
                Latino/Latina ☐
                Asian ☐
                Native American ☐
                Other ☐

A3. What language did you first learn to speak? _____

A4. Where were you born? _____

A5. How many years have you lived in the United States? _____

A6. Age: ____

A7. Grade: ____

A8. Years at _____ Middle School:_____

B1. Please think about your life at _____ Middle School and tell us how each of the statements describes your perception of your experience. Circle your answers.

	Very much	Somewhat	Not really	Not at all	Don't know
a. The school is a safe place.	1	2	3	4	5
b. I am treated fairly in school.	1	2	3	4	5
c. I get the extra help in school that I need.	1	2	3	4	5
d. I think that schoolwork is important.	1	2	3	4	5
e. Teachers assign work that is hard enough for me.	1	2	3	4	5
f. Teachers assign work that is too hard for me.	1	2	3	4	5
g. Teachers and other staff respect me.	1	2	3	4	5
h. The school encourages my family to be involved in events at the school.	1	2	3	4	5
i. Teachers and other staff at the school care about me.	1	2	3	4	5
k. I feel like I belong in this school.	1	2	3	4	5
l. In my classes, students are encouraged to work collaboratively.	1	2	3	4	5
m. I am encouraged to think rather than to memorize facts.	1	2	3	4	5
n. In my classes I learn to apply my knowledge to everyday life through community service projects.	1	2	3	4	5

B2. Please think about your experiences at _____ Middle School and tell if you agree, disagree, or neither agree nor disagree with the following statement.

	Strongly agree	Agree	Neither agree nor disagree	Disagree	Strongly disagree
a. School is boring.	1	2	3	4	5
b. When I wake up in the morning, I often don't feel like going to school.	1	2	3	4	5
c. I feel like I don't know a lot of kids in this school.	1	2	3	4	5
d. I feel like my teachers don't know me very well.	1	2	3	4	5
e. Adults in this school treat students the same no matter which gender they are.	1	2	3	4	5
f. Adults in this school treat students the same no matter what race they are.	1	2	3	4	5
g. Adults in this school really listen to what you have to say.	1	2	3	4	5
h. There is no point in doing well in school.	1	2	3	4	5
i. I would like to have a close friend of another race.	1	2	3	4	5

B3. Please think about life at _____ Middle School and tell us how often each of the following happens.

	All the time	Most of the time	About half the time	Once in a while	Never
a. When you work hard on schoolwork, how often do teachers praise your work?	1	2	3	4	5
b. How often do you feel left out when you are at school?	1	2	3	4	5
c. Are there times you do not feel safe in this school?	1	2	3	4	5
d. When students in this school are having problems, how often do they get an adult to help them work the problems out?	1	2	3	4	5
e. How often do you worry about getting beaten up at school?	1	2	3	4	5
f. I prefer to spend time with people like myself.	1	2	3	4	5
g. I am comfortable being in a group where everybody is of another race.	1	2	3	4	5
h. When people say bad things about people of another race, I get angry.	1	2	3	4	5
i. When people pick on me, I think that it is because of my race.	1	2	3	4	5
j. How often do students fight during school?	1	2	3	4	5

	All the time	Most of the time	About half the time	Once in a while	Never
k. How often are students in your school recognized or given awards for contributions to the school or community?	1	2	3	4	5

B4. Please think about your experience of life at _____ Middle School and tell us how each of the statements describes your perception of your experience.

	A lot	Pretty much	Some	Not very much	Not at all
a. How much do the adults in this school care about you as a person?	1	2	3	4	5
b. How proud do you feel of your school?	1	2	3	4	5

B5. Please think about the teachers and students at _____ Middle School and tell us how each of the statements describes your perception of your experience.

	All	Most	About half	A few	None
a. How many of the teachers you know in this school think it is very important for their students to learn their schoolwork?	1	2	3	4	5
b. How many students in this school try hard to get good grades?	1	2	3	4	5
c. How many students would defend the school when bad things are said about it?	1	2	3	4	5

B6. Please think about how much of a problem each of the following is at
_____ Middle School.

	No problem	Minor problem	Moderate problem	Serious problem
a. Student vandalism or theft.	1	2	3	4
b. Student disrespect for teachers.	1	2	3	4
c. Substance abuse by students.	1	2	3	4

C1. How far in school do you think you will get?

Will attend school until 16 years old. ☐
Will graduate from high school. ☐
Will graduate from vocational or trade or business school
  after high school. ☐
Will graduate from college. ☐
Will go to graduate school. ☐

TEACHER SURVEY

Please Tell Us About Yourself.

A1. Number of years teaching experience: _____

A2. Number of years teaching at this school: _____

A3. Gender: Male ☐   Female ☐

A4. Race

African American ☐
Caucasian ☐
Latino/Latina ☐
Asian ☐
Native American ☐
Other ☐

B1. Please think about your experience of life at _____ Middle School and tell us how each of the statements describes your perception of your experience.

	Very much	Somewhat	Not really	Not at all	Don't know
a. The school is a safe place.	1	2	3	4	5
b. Children are treated fairly in school.	1	2	3	4	5
c. Children get the extra help in school that they need.	1	2	3	4	5
d. Students at the school understand that schoolwork is important.	1	2	3	4	5
e. Teachers assign work that is hard enough for students.	1	2	3	4	5
f. Teachers assign work that is too hard for students.	1	2	3	4	5
g. Teachers and other staff respect parents at the school.	1	2	3	4	5
h. Children are respected by the teachers and staff.	1	2	3	4	5

	Very much	Somewhat	Not really	Not at all	Don't know
i. The school encourages parents to be involved in events at the school.	1	2	3	4	5
j. Teachers and other staff at the school care about all children.	1	2	3	4	5
k. Students feel like they belong in this school.	1	2	3	4	5

B2. Thinking about _____ Middle School, tell us how much you agree with the following statements.

	Strongly disagree	Disagree	Neutral	Agree	Strongly agree
a. The school curriculum provides opportunities for nurturing students' curiosity.	1	2	3	4	5
b. The curriculum includes core knowledge, concepts, (and facts) in each curriculum area.	1	2	3	4	5
c. The curriculum promotes an appreciation of cultural and intellectual diversity.	1	2	3	4	5
d. There is support for many different kinds of learning styles.	1	2	3	4	5
e. The instructional approach develops children's confidence to engage in independent thinking.	1	2	3	4	5
f. The instructional approach helps students to work collaboratively.	1	2	3	4	5

	Strongly disagree	Disagree	Neutral	Agree	Strongly agree
g. Students are encouraged to think rather than to memorize facts.	1	2	3	4	5
h. Students learn to apply their knowledge to everyday life through community service projects.	1	2	3	4	5
i. Teachers and staff hold high academic expectations for all students.	1	2	3	4	5
j. Teachers and staff hold high behavioral expectations for all students.	1	2	3	4	5
k. The school keeps order and discipline among the students.	1	2	3	4	5
l. There is a strong sense of academic purpose and support for academic skills.	1	2	3	4	5
m. There are clearly articulated standards for student performance, which are communicated to students and families.	1	2	3	4	5
n. The needs of special education students are met within the least restrictive environment.	1	2	3	4	5
o. Students are known as individuals to adults in the school and receive positive, nurturing attention.	1	2	3	4	5

	Strongly disagree	Disagree	Neutral	Agree	Strongly agree
p. Time is structured within the school day to maximize student learning.	1	2	3	4	5
q. The school focuses on activities and curriculum that will create lifelong learners.	1	2	3	4	5
r. Adults in this school treat students the same no matter what race they are.	1	2	3	4	5
s. Adults in this school treat students the same no matter what gender they are.	1	2	3	4	5
t. Students in this school mainly have friends of the same race	1	2	3	4	5

C1. Please think about your experience as a teacher at _____ Middle School and tell us how each of the statements describes your experience.

	Strongly agree	Agree	Neither agree nor disagree	Disagree
a. Routine duties and paperwork interfere with my job.	1	2	3	4
b. There is a great deal of cooperative effort among staff members.	1	2	3	4
c. The level of student misbehavior in this school interferes with my job.	1	2	3	4
d. Rules for student behavior are consistently enforced by staff in this school, even for students who are not in their classes.	1	2	3	4

	Strongly agree	Agree	Neither agree nor disagree	Disagree
e. I usually look forward to working each day at this school.	1	2	3	4
f. My school's administration sets priorities in consultation with other school staff.	1	2	3	4
g. Teachers in this school are continually learning and seeking new ideas.	1	2	3	4
h. Staff maintain high academic standards.	1	2	3	4
i. Staff members in this school generally do not have much school spirit.	1	2	3	4
j. School administrators know the problems faced by school staff.	1	2	3	4
k. The attitudes and habits students bring to this school greatly reduce their chances for academic success.	1	2	3	4
l. Many of the students in this school are not capable of learning the material the school is supposed to teach them.	1	2	3	4

C2. Please think about your experience as a teacher at _____ Middle School and tell us how much of a problem each issue is at your school.

	Not a problem	Minor problem	Moderate problem	Serious problem
a. Student absenteeism.	1	2	3	4
b. Student tardiness or class cutting.	1	2	3	4
c. Teacher absenteeism.	1	2	3	4
d. Student mobility.	1	2	3	4
e. Physical conflict among students.	1	2	3	4

	Not a problem	Minor problem	Moderate problem	Serious problem
f. Student vandalism or theft.	1	2	3	4
g. Student disrespect for teachers.	1	2	3	4
h. Lack of parental supervision.	1	2	3	4
i. Inadequate rest or nutrition among students.	1	2	3	4
j. Substance abuse by students' family members.	1	2	3	4
k. Substance abuse by students.	1	2	3	4
l. Student apathy.	1	2	3	4

D1. How far in school do you think most students in this school will get?

Will attend school until 16 years old. ☐
Will graduate from high school. ☐
Will graduate from vocational or trade or business school
   after high school. ☐
Will graduate from college. ☐
Will go to graduate school ☐

E1. In which of the following areas have you received staff development in the past 12 months? (*Please circle all that apply.*)

a. Instruction for students with special needs

b. Content-area instruction

c. Effective models of teaching

d. Cooperative learning

e. Learning styles

f. Classroom management strategies

g. Effective schools research and application

h. Schoolwide discipline policy

i. Change through consensus decision making

j. Elements of a shared vision

k. School-based management

l. Parental involvement

m. Integration of supplemental services

n. Social skills

o. Other *(Please specify)*

E2. Look at the list above. In which of these areas, if any, do you particularly wish professional development that you have *not* received (use the back of the page if necessary).

E3. To what extent does this school have effective staff development for all staff?

Not at all				A great deal
1	2	3	4	5

E4. To what extent is the staff development plan modified through recommendations from staff and parents?

Not at all				A great deal
1	2	3	4	5

E5. To what extent did staff development offered in the past 12 months meet your needs as a teacher?

Not at all				A great deal
1	2	3	4	5

E6. Have you participated in any of the following in the past 12 months? *(Circle all that apply.)*

a. Developing a personal professional development plan.

b. Visiting other classrooms to observe

c. Visiting other schools to observe

d. Participating in a teacher study group

e. Designing a staff development event

E7. Look at the list above. Which of these do you think would most interest you? (List only one.)

PARENT SURVEY

Dear Parent: Please complete this for your child who attends _____
Middle School. If you have more than one child at _____ Middle
School, please complete it for your *oldest* child.

A1. Child's Gender: Male ☐   Female ☐

A2. Race

African American ☐
Caucasian ☐
Latino/Latina ☐
Asian ☐
Native American ☐
Other ☐

A3. What language do you speak at home?_____

A4. Child's age: _____

A5. Child's grade: _____

A6. How many years has your child attended _____ Middle
School?_____

A7. Is your child currently receiving special education services?
        Yes ☐   No ☐

If so, what services does he or she receive:

A8. How many times have you moved in the past 2 years? _____

A9. Do any of your other children attend _____ Middle School?
        Yes ☐   No ☐

If yes, what grade are they in? _____

B1. Please think about the school experience your child at _____
Middle School this year since September, and tell us how each of the statements
describes your child's school experience.

	Very much	Somewhat	Not really	Not at all	Don't know
a. The school is a safe place.	1	2	3	4	5
b. My child is treated fairly in school.	1	2	3	4	5
c. My child gets the extra help in school if he/she needs it.	1	2	3	4	5
d. The students at the school understand that schoolwork is important.	1	2	3	4	5
e. The teachers give my child schoolwork that is hard enough for him/her.	1	2	3	4	5
f. The schoolwork my child gets is *too* hard for him/her.	1	2	3	4	5
g. I am respected by the teachers and others at the school.	1	2	3	4	5
h. My child is respected by the teachers.	1	2	3	4	5
i. The school encourages parents to be involved in events at the school.	1	2	3	4	5
j. The teachers and other people at the school care about my child.	1	2	3	4	5
k. My child feels like he/she belongs in this school.	1	2	3	4	5

B2. Thinking about _____ Middle School, tell us how much you agree with the following statements.

	Strongly disagree	Disagree	Neutral	Agree	Strongly agree
a. I am comfortable meeting with my child's teachers.	1	2	3	4	5
b. It is easy to make appointments with the teachers, guidance counselor, or principal.	1	2	3	4	5
c. The school makes it easy for me to talk to someone if I am worried about my child.	1	2	3	4	5
d. The school lets me know when there are meetings or other events going on.	1	2	3	4	5
e. The school makes me feel welcome when I visit.	1	2	3	4	5
f. If I could choose, I would still choose this school for my child.	1	2	3	4	5
g. My child's teachers view me as a partner or team member in educating my child.	1	2	3	4	5
h. The school staff understand the problems I face as a parent.	1	2	3	4	5

B3. Thinking about teaching and learning at _____ Middle School, tell us how much you agree with the following statements.

	Strongly disagree	Disagree	Neutral	Agree	Strongly agree
a. The school curriculum provides opportunities for nurturing my child's curiosity, sensitivity, and appreciation (of what?).	1	2	3	4	5
b. The curriculum includes core knowledge, concepts, (and facts) in each curriculum area.	1	2	3	4	5
c. The curriculum promotes an appreciation of cultural and intellectual diversity.	1	2	3	4	5
d. There is support for many different kinds of learning styles.	1	2	3	4	5
e. The instructional approach develops my child's confidence to engage in independent thinking.	1	2	3	4	5
f. The instructional approach helps students to work together collaboratively.	1	2	3	4	5
g. Students are encouraged to think rather than to memorize facts.	1	2	3	4	5
h. Students learn to apply their knowledge to everyday life through community service projects.	1	2	3	4	5
i. Teachers and staff hold high academic expectations for all students.	1	2	3	4	5

	Strongly disagree	Disagree	Neutral	Agree	Strongly agree
j. Teachers and staff hold high behavioral expectations for all students.	1	2	3	4	5
k. The school keeps order and discipline among the children.	1	2	3	4	5
l. There is a strong sense of academic purpose and support for academic skills.	1	2	3	4	5
m. There are clearly standards for student performance, which are communicated to students and families.	1	2	3	4	5
n. The needs of special education students are met within the least restrictive environment.	1	2	3	4	5
o. Students are known as individuals to adults in the school and receive positive, nurturing attention.	1	2	3	4	5
p. Time is structured within the school day to maximize student learning.	1	2	3	4	5
q. The school focuses on activities and curricula that will create lifelong learners.	1	2	3	4	5

C1. How far in school do you think your child will get?

Will attend school until 16 years old.   □
Will graduate from high school.   □
Will graduate from vocational or trade or business school
    after high school.   □
Will graduate from college.   □
Will go to graduate school.   □

Notes

Chapter 2

1. Since the late 1960s, a number of educational researchers and writers have focused on the migrant lifestyle and its effects on children's learning (Altman, 1994; Bowe, 2003). Literature such as Steinbeck's classic *The Grapes of Wrath* and Grisham's *Painted House* and *The Circuit* depict the migrant lifestyle at different historical periods and with different migrant groups and settings.

Chapter 3

1. Hispanic students are a large and growing segment of the U.S. student population. The proportion of the U.S. student population that is Latino has doubled in the past 20 years, from 8.6% in 1980 to 16.2% in 1999 (and is nearly triple the 1973 proportion of 5.7%). Most come from relatively impoverished developing countries and from low socioeconomic strata within those countries (National Council of La Raza, 2001). Nationwide, 50% of all immigrants are from Latin America (Suarez-Orozco, 2001). While immigration offers an opportunity to develop the skills and education they need, Latino students consistently underachieve in comparison with other students. At the age of 17, only one in 50 Latinos can read and gain information from specialized text, such as the science section in a newspaper. One out of every 10 Latino students drops out of high school before graduation, compared with one out of 30 White students. And Latino students obtain college degrees at only half the rate of White students (Haycock & Huang, 2001). Da Vinci faculty members say they are committed to changing those statistics.

2. The early impact of Project Explore has been well chronicled by the Center for Children and Technology (CCT) of Education Development Center, Inc. in New York City, with research funding support from the National Science Foundation. The project accomplished the following:

- Changed the way students go about learning
- Helped to raise standardized achievement scores of Da Vinci students
- Contributed to improved academic performance overall in the feeder high school when the Project Explore students entered 2 years later

CCT also documented an improvement in achievement scores of the Project Explore students as they progressed through Da Vinci and on through the high school. But it was not only the Project Explore students whose academic scores improved dramatically; scores increased for all students in the feeder high school. High school teachers found that, more often than in previous years, student work habits and achievement scores improved. The CCT staff interpret these results as evidence that this technology-supported learning can, over time, change teachers' expectations for their students—and thus student achievement—in general (Honey, 1999).

Appendix A

1. We adapted the majority of items from surveys developed by Dr. Thomas Cook of Northwestern University and his colleagues for evaluations of the Comer School Development program in Chicago, Cleveland, and Detroit. We drew additional items from the Schools and Staffing Survey, developed by the U.S. Department of Education, National Center for Education Statistics.

2. Shadowing derives from anthropology and was adapted by the Johns Hopkins University and Abt Associates, Inc., in 1992 as part of a 3-year study of Title I schools. Students' perspectives rarely are included in any detail in descriptions and analyses of educational programs. As a result, valuable information about how and why particular instructional practices work, which might help practitioners use new practices successfully, is excluded (Knapp, Shields, & Turnbull, 1993; Means & Knapp, 1991; Rowan, Guthrie, Lee, & Guthrie, 1986).

References

Alliance for Excellent Education. (2005a, February 14). Bush spending plan cuts education by 0.9 percent overall: $1.5 billion plan for high schools paid for through cuts totaling $2.17 billion. *Straight A's, 5*(3), 1–5.

Alliance for Excellent Education. (2005b, February 28). Achieve and NGA host National Education Summit on High Schools: Governors, educators, and business leaders meet to discuss high school reform. *Straight A's, 5*(4), 1–2.

Altman, L. J. (1994). *Migrant farm workers: The temporary people*. New York: Franklin Watts.

Anfara, V., Brown, K. M., & Mangione, T. L. (2002). Qualitative analysis on stage: Making the research process more public. *Educational Researcher, 31*(7), 28–38.

Behn, R. D. (1988). Management by groping along. *Journal of Policy Analysis and Management, 7*(4), 643–663.

Biesta, G. J. J., & Burbules, N. C. (2003). *Pragmatism and educational research*. Lanham, MD: Rowman & Littlefield.

Blythe, T., Allen, D., & Powell, B. S. (1999). *Looking together at student work: A companion guide to assessing student learning*. New York: Teachers College Press.

Bowe, J. (2003, April 21 and 28). Nobodies: Does slavery exist in modern America? *The New Yorker, 79*(9), 106–108ff.

Bransford, J., Brown, A., & Cocking, R. (Eds.). (2000). *How people learn: Brain, mind, experience, and school* (Expanded ed.). Washington, DC: National Academy of Sciences, National Research Council.

Brigham, N., & Rosenblum, S. (1998). *Innovations, retrovations, and reservations: The study of innovations in Massachusetts charter schools*. Report to the Massachusetts Department of Education, Boston.

Brown, A., & Campione, J. C. (1994). Guided discovery in a community of learners. In K. McGilly (Ed.), *Classroom lessons: Integrating cognitive theory and classroom practice* (pp. 229–270). Cambridge, MA: MIT Press/Bradford Books.

Brown, A., & Campione, J. C. (1996). Psychological theory and the design of innovative learning environments: On procedures, principles, and systems. In L. Schauble & R. Glaser (Eds.), *Innovations in learning: New environments in education* (pp. 289–325). Mahwah, NJ: Erlbaum.

Bryk, A. S., & Schneider, B. (2002). *Trust in schools: A core resource for improvement*. New York: Russell Sage.

Caine, G., & Caine, R. M. (1994). *Mindshifts: A brain-based process for restructuring schools and renewing education*. Tucson, AZ: Zephr Press.

Callins, T. (2004). *Culturally responsive literacy instruction* (Practitioner Brief Series). National Center for Culturally Responsive Educational Systems. Retrieved March 18, 2005 from http://www.nccrest.org/publications_briefs.html

Campbell, J. R., Voelkl, K. E., & Donahue, P. L. (1997). *NAEP 1996 trends in academic progress.* Washington, DC: National Center for Education Statistics.

Carnegie Council on Adolescent Development. (1989). *Turning points: Preparing American youth for the 21st century.* New York: Carnegie Corporation of New York.

Coben, S. S., Thomas, C. C., Sattler, R. O., & Morsink, C. V. (1997). Meeting the challenge of consultation and collaboration: Developing interactive teams. *Journal of Learning Disabilities, 30,* 427–432.

Coburn, C. E. (2001). Collective sensemaking about reading: How teachers mediate reading policy in their professional communities. *Educational Evaluation and Policy Analysis, 23*(2), 145–170.

Comer, J. P., Haynes, N. M., Joyner, E. T., & Ben-Avie, M. (Eds.). (1996). *Rallying the whole village: The Comer process for reforming education.* New York: Teachers College Press.

Cook, L., & Friend, M. (1995). Co-teaching: Guidelines for creating effective practices. *Focus on Exceptional Children, 28,* 1–16.

Cushman, K. (1990a). Performances and exhibitions: The demonstration of mastery. *Horace, 6*(3). Retrieved March 28, 2005, from http://www.essentialschools.org/cs/resources/view/ces_res/138

Cushman, K. (1990b). Are advisory groups "essential"? What they do, how they work. *Horace, 7*(1). Retrieved March 28, 2005, from http://www. essentialschools.org/cs/resources/view/ces_res/8

Darling-Hammond, L. (2004). From "Separate but Equal" to "No Child Left Behind": The collision of new standards and old inequalities. In D. Meier & G. Wood (Eds.), *Many children left behind: How the No Child Left Behind Act is damaging our children and our schools* (pp. 3–32). Boston: Beacon Press.

Delpit, L. (1995). *Other people's children: Cultural conflict in the classroom.* New York: New Press.

DeWind, J. (1998). *Addressing the plight of migrant workers in the United States and Asia: Opportunities and challenges in applying human rights standards.* Carnegie Council on Ethics and International Affairs. Retrieved March 16, 2005 from http://www.carnegiecouncil.org/viewMedia.php/prmTemplateID/8/prmID/595

Dieker, L. A. (2001). What are the characteristics of "effective" middle and high school co-taught teams for students with disabilities? *Preventing School Failure, 46*(1), 14–23.

Dufour, R. (2001). In the right context. *Journal of Staff Development, 22*(1), 14–17.

Education Development Center. (1994). *Documentation of the national middle-grades reform: The conversations.* Unpublished documents.

Education Trust. (2005, January). *Stalled in secondary: A look at student achievement since the No Child Left Behind Act.* Oakland, CA: Author. Retrieved March 29, 2005 from http://www2.edtrust.org/edtrust/Product+Catalog/special+reports

Elmore, R. (1996). Getting to scale with good educational practice. *Harvard Education Review, 66*(1), 1–24.

Englert, C. S., Garmon, A., Mariage, T., Rozendal, M., Tarrant, K., & Urba, J. (1995). The early literacy project: Connecting across the literacy curriculum. *Learning Disability Quarterly, 18*, 253–275.

Frechtling, J., & Sharp, L. (1997). *User-friendly handbook for mixed method evaluations.* Arlington, VA: National Science Foundation, Directorate for Education and Human Resources, Division of Research, Evaluation and Communication.

Freivogel, W. H. (2001). *St. Louis: Desegregation and school choice in the land of Dred Scott.* Unpublished report by the Spencer Foundation, Chicago.

Fuchs, L. S., Fuchs, D., Hamlett, C. L., Phillips, N. B., Karns, K., & Dutka, S. (1997). Enhancing students' helping behavior during peer mediated instruction with conceptual mathematics explanations. *Elementary School Journal, 97*, 223–249.

Fullan, M. (2003). *The moral imperative of school leadership.* Thousand Oaks, CA: Corwin Press.

Gardner, H. (1999). *Intelligence reframed: Multiple intelligences for the 21st century.* New York: Basic Books.

Geertz, C. (1973). *The interpretation of cultures.* New York: Basic Books.

Guba, E. G., & Lincoln, Y. S. (1994). Competing paradigms in qualitative research. In N. K. Denzin & Y. S. Lincoln (Eds.), *Handbook of qualitative research* (pp. 105–117). Thousand Oaks, CA: Sage.

Guthrie, J. T., & Alvermann, D. A. (Eds.). (1999). *Engaged reading: Processes, practices and policy implications.* New York: Teachers College Press.

Haycock, K., & Huang, S. (2001). Are today's high school graduates ready? *Thinking K-16, 5*(1). Retrieved March 18, 2005 from www.ed.gov/about/offices/list/ovae/pi/hs/edtrust.doc

Hilliard, A., III. (2002). Cultural pluralism in education. In D. Dickinson (Ed.), *Creating the future: Perspectives on educational change* (pp. 96–102). Seattle: New Horizons for Learning. Retrieved March 24, 2005, from http://www.newhorizons.org/future/Creating_the_Future/crfut_hilliard.html

Hobbs, T., & Westling, D. L. (1998). Promoting successful inclusion through collaborative problem-solving. *Teaching Exceptional Children, 31*, 12–19.

Honey, M. (1999). *Union City school reform.* Unpublished paper presented at the Harvard Graduate School of Education, Summer Institute of the Urban Special Education Leadership Collaborative. Report developed by the Center for Children and Technology, Education Development Center, Inc., New York.

Honig, M. I. (2004). Where's the "up" in bottom-up reform? *Educational Policy, 18*(4), 527–561.

Honig, M. I., & Hatch, T. C. (2004). Crafting coherence: How schools strategically manage multiple, external demands. *Educational Researcher, 33*(8), 16–30.

Irvin, J. L. (1995). Cognitive growth during early adolescence: The regulator of developmental tasks. *Middle School Journal, 27*(1), 54–55.

Janney, R. E., Snell, M. E., Beers, M. K., & Raynes, M. (1995). Integrating students with moderate and severe disabilities into general education classes. *Exceptional Children, 61*, 423–439.

Johnson, D. W., Johnson, R. T., & Holubec, E. J. (1994). *The new circles of learning:*

Cooperation in the classroom and school. Alexandria, VA: Association for Supervision and Curriculum Development.

Johnson, R. B., & Onwuegbuzie, A. J. (2004). Mixed methods research: A research paradigm whose time has come. *Educational Researcher, 33*(7), 27–31.

Johnson, R. N. (1996). Kant's conception of merit. *Pacific Philosophical Quarterly, 77*, 313–337.

Kanter, R. M. (1988). When a thousand flowers bloom: Structural, collective, and social conditions for innovation in organizations. *Research in Organizational Behavior, 10*, 169–211.

Knapp, M. S., Shields, P. M., & Turnbull, B. J. (1993). *Academic challenge for the children of poverty.* Washington, DC: U.S. Department of Education.

Ladson-Billings, G. (1994). *The dreamkeepers: Successful teachers of African-American children.* San Francisco: Jossey-Bass.

Ladson-Billings, G. (2001). *Crossing over to Canaan: The journey of new teachers in diverse classrooms.* San Francisco: Jossey-Bass.

Lave, J. (1991). Situated learning in communities of practice. In L. B. Resnick, J. M. Levine, & S. D. Teasley (Eds.), *Perspectives on socially shared cognition* (pp. 63–82). Washington, DC: American Psychological Association.

Levins, H. (1994, May 15). Black, white and brown. *St. Louis Post-Dispatch*, p. B4.

Lipsitz, J. (1984). *Successful schools for young adolescents.* Westerville, OH: National Middle School Association.

Lipsitz, J., Mizell, M. H., Jackson, A., & Austin, L. M. (1997). Speaking with one voice. A manifesto for middle grades reform. *Phi Delta Kappan, 78*(7), 533–540.

Little, T. S., & Dacus, N. B. (1999). Looping: Moving up with the class. *Educational Leadership, 57*, 42–45.

Louis, K. S., Kruse, S. D., & Marks, H. M. (1996). Schoolwide professional community: Teachers' work, intellectual quality, and commitment. In F. M. Newmann & Associates (Eds.), *Authentic achievement: Restructuring schools for intellectual quality* (pp. 179–204). San Francisco: Jossey-Bass.

MacIver, D. J. (1990). Meeting the needs of young adolescents: Advisory groups, interdisciplinary teaching teams, and school transition programs. *Phi Delta Kappan, 71*(6), 458–464.

MacIver, D. J., & Epstein, J. L. (1993). Middle grades research: Not yet mature, but no longer a child. *Elementary School Journal, 93*(5), 519–533.

McCombs, J. S., Kirby, S. N., Barney, H., Darilek, H., & Magee, S. (2004). *Achieving state and national literacy goals, a long uphill road: A report to Carnegie Corporation of New York.* Santa Monica, CA: RAND.

McDonald, J. P. (1996). *Designing schools.* San Francisco: Jossey-Bass.

McKinney, J. D., Montague, M., & Hocutt, A. M. (1998, April). *A two year follow-up study of children at risk for developing SED: Implications for designing prevention programs.* Paper presented at the annual convention of the Council for Exceptional Children, Minneapolis.

McLaughlin, M. W., & Talbert, J. E. (2001). *Professional communities and the work of high school teaching.* Chicago: University of Chicago Press.

Means, B., Chelemer, C., & Knapp, M. S. (Eds.). (1991). *Teaching advanced skills to at-risk students: Views from research and practice.* San Francisco: Jossey-Bass.

Means, B., & Knapp, M. S. (1991). Introduction: Rethinking teaching for disadvantaged students. In B. Means, C. Chelemer, & M. S. Knapp (Eds.), *Teaching advanced skills to at-risk students: Views from research and practice* (pp. 1–27). San Francisco: Jossey-Bass.

Meier, D. (2004). NCLB and democracy. In D. Meier & G. Wood (Eds.), *Many children left behind: How the No Child Left Behind Act is damaging our children and our schools* (pp. 66–78). Boston: Beacon Press.

Miles, M. B., & Huberman, A. M. (1994). *Qualitative data analysis* (2nd ed.). Thousand Oaks, CA: Sage.

Morey, A., & Kilano, M. (1997). *Multicultural course transformation in higher education: A broader truth.* Needham Heights, MA: Allyn & Bacon.

Morocco, C. C., & Aguilar, C. M. (2002). Co-teaching for content understanding: A schoolwide model. *Journal of Educational and Psychological Consultation, 13*(4), 315–347.

Morocco, C. C., Clark-Chiarelli, N., & Aguilar, C. M. (2002). Cultures of excellence and belonging in urban middle schools. *Research in Middle Level Education Online, 25*(2).

Morocco, C. C., Hindin, A., & Aguilar, C. M. (2002). The role of conversation in a thematic understanding of literature. *Learning Disabilities Research and Practice, 17*, 144–157.

Morocco, C. C., Walker, A., & Lewis, L. (2003). Access to the schoolwide thinking curriculum. *Journal of Special Education Leadership, 16*(1), 5–14.

Murawski, W. W., & Swanson, H. L. (2001). A meta-analysis of co-teaching research: Where are the data? *Remedial and Special Education, 22*(5), 258–267.

National Association of Secondary School Principals. (2005). *NASSP legislative recommendations for high school reform.* Reston, VA: Author.

National Council of La Raza. (2001, August). *Beyond the census: Hispanics and an American agenda.* Washington, DC: Author. Available at www.nclr.org

National Council of Teachers of English and International Reading Association. (1996). *Standards for the English language arts.* Urbana, IL, & Newark, DE: Author.

National Council of Teachers of Mathematics. (1989). *Curriculum and evaluation standards for school mathematics.* Reston, VA: Author.

National Middle School Association. (1995). *This we believe: Developmentally responsive middle level schools.* Westerville, OH: Author.

National Science Foundation. (1997). *Foundations: The challenge and promise of K–8 science education reform.* Arlington, VA: National Science Foundation, Directorate for Education and Human Resources, Division of Elementary, Secondary, and Informal Education.

Nave, B. (2000). *Critical friends groups: Their impact on students, teachers, and schools.* Bloomington, IN: Annenberg Institute for School Reform.

Newmann, F. M., & Associates (Eds.). (1996). *Authentic achievement: Restructuring schools for intellectual quality.* San Francisco: Jossey-Bass.

Newmann, F. M., & Wehlage, G. G. (1995). *Successful school restructuring.* Madison, WI: Center on the Organization and Restructuring of Schools.

Nieto, S. (1996). *Affirming diversity: The sociopolitical context of multicultural education.* White Plains, NY: Longman.

Noguera, P. A. (2003). Joaquin's dilemma: Understanding the link between racial identity and school-related behaviors. In M. Sadowski (Ed.), *Adolescents at school: Perspectives on youth, identity, and education.* Cambridge, MA: Harvard University Press.

Palincsar, A. S., & Klenk, L. (1992). Fostering literacy learning in supportive contexts. *Journal of Learning Disabilities, 25,* 211–225.

Palincsar, A. S., Magnusson, S. M., Marano, N. L., Ford, D., & Brown, N. M. (1998). Designing a community of practice: Principles and practices of the GIsML community. *Teaching and Teacher Education, 14*(1), 5–19.

Palincsar, A. S., & Rupert-Herrenkohl, K. (1999). Designing collaborative contexts: Lessons from three research programs. In A. O'Donnell & A. King (Eds.), *Cognitive perspectives on peer learning* (pp. 151–178). Mahwah, NJ: Erlbaum.

Patton, M. Q. (2001). *Qualitative research & evaluation methods* (3rd ed.). Thousand Oaks, CA: Sage.

RAND Reading Study Group. (2002). *Reading for understanding: Toward an R&D program in reading comprehension.* Santa Monica, CA: RAND.

Rice, D., & Zigmond, N. (2000). Co-teaching in secondary schools: Teacher reports of developments in Australian and American classrooms. *Learning Disabilities Research & Practice, 15,* 190–197.

Rowan, B. L., Guthrie, F., Lee, G. V., & Guthrie, G. P. (1986). *The design and implementation of Chapter 1 instructional services: A study of 24 schools* (Final report for Office of Educational Research and Improvement, U.S. Department of Education, contract no. 400-85-1015). San Francisco: Far West Laboratory for Educational Research and Development.

Sapolsky, R. M. (1998). *Why zebras don't get ulcers: A guide to stress, stress-related disease and coping* (2nd ed.). New York: W. H. Freeman.

Showers, B., & Joyce, B. (1996). The evolution of peer coaching. *Educational Leadership, 53*(6), 12–16.

Silva, P., & Mackin, R. A. (2002). *Standards of mind and heart: Creating the good high school.* New York: Teachers College Press.

Suarez-Orozco, C., & Suarez-Orozco, M. M. (1995). *Transformations, immigration, family life, and achievement motivation among Latino adolescents.* Stanford: Stanford University Press.

Suarez-Orozco, C., & Suarez-Orozco, M. M. (2001). *Children of immigration: The developing child.* Cambridge, MA: Harvard University Press.

Suarez-Orozco, M. M. (2001). Globalization, immigration, and education: The research agenda. *Harvard Education Review, 71*(3), 345–365.

Swiderek, B. (1997). Full inclusion—making it work. *Journal of Adolescent and Adult Literacy, 41,* 234–235.

Tanner, C. K. (1996). Inclusive education in the United States: Beliefs and practices among middle school principals and teachers. *Educational Policy Archives, 4,* 1–30.

Tashakkori, A., & Teddlie, C. (1998). *Mixed methodology: Combining qualitative and quantitative approaches* (Applied Social Research Methods Series, Vol. 46). London: Sage.

Vaughn, S., Gersten, R., & Chard, D. J. (2000). The underlying message in LD intervention research: Findings from research syntheses. *Exceptional Children, 67*(1), 99–114.

Vaughn, S., Schumm, J. S., & Arguelles, M. E. (1997). The ABCDEs of co-teaching. *Teaching Exceptional Children, 30*(2), 1–10.

Viadero, D. (1996, January 17). Mix and match: The experimental Schools for Thought combines three promising cognitive learning approaches to promote deep and true understanding. *Education Week*. Retrieved March 28, 2005 from http://www.edweek.org/ew/articles/1996/01/17/17think.h15.html

Walther-Thomas, C. S. (1997). Co-teaching experiences: The benefits and problems that teachers and principals report over time. *Journal of Learning Disabilities, 30*, 395–407.

Walther-Thomas, C. S., Bryant, M., & Land, S. (1996). Planning for effective co-teaching. *Remedial and Special Education, 17*, 255–264.

Williams, J. P. (1998). Improving the comprehension of disabled readers. *Annals of Dyslexia, 48*, 213–238.

Williamson, R., & Johnston, J. H. (1999). Challenging orthodoxy: An emerging agenda for middle level reform. *Middle School Journal, 30*(4), 10–17.

Wong, B. Y. L., Butler, D. L., Ficzere, S. A., & Kuperis, S. (1996). Teaching adolescents with learning disabilities and low achievers to plan, write, and revise compare-and-contrast essays. *Learning Disabilities Research and Practice, 12*(1), 2–15.

Woodward, J., Baxter, J., & Robinson, R. (1999). Rules and reasons: Decimal instruction for academically low achieving students. *Learning Disabilities Research and Practice, 14*(1), 15–24.

Zigmond, N. (2001). Special education at the crossroads. *Preventing School Failure, 45*, 70-74.

Zigmond, N., & Magiera, K. (2001). A focus on co-teaching: Use caution. *Current Practice Alerts, 6*(6). Retrieved March 16, 2005 from http://www.dldcec.org/pdf/Alert6.pdf

Index

About the Authors

Catherine Cobb Morocco, a senior scientist at Education Development Center, Inc. (EDC), directs research and development programs aimed at improving middle and high schools, particularly in the area of literacy. One area of her work focuses on constituting professional communities that improve literacy instruction and improve outcomes for students with disabilities. She directed the REACH Institute, a collaboration with three universities to study classroom interventions in the major disciplines that support high-risk students in learning challenging content. She is a senior author of *Supported Literacy*™—a school wide approach to assessment, reading foundations, and comprehension and composing for academically diverse classrooms. Another area of her work involves unearthing important practices and models in existing schools. She is currently working with the other authors on studying high-performing high schools and successful parent involvement programs. She has taught middle and high school students, undergraduates, and graduate students, and holds a doctorate from Harvard University.

Nancy Brigham is actively engaged in education research, both as a consultant and as a partner in her own firm, Rosenblum Brigham Associates (RBA). She began her career in education as a teacher of emotionally disturbed blind children in a private institution and then became a public elementary school teacher. For the past 25 years, she has been involved in national studies of education programs for Abt Associates in Cambridge, MA, and Cosmos Corporation in Washington, DC. Her affiliation with EDC spans many years and projects, including evaluations conducted for the National Forum to Accelerate Middle Grades Reform, the Department of Education, and the National Science Foundation. She is the author of myriad reports and a frequent presenter at national conferences. In 1994, she was an invited participant at a Wingspread Conference on issues of education reform.

Cynthia Mata Aguilar brings 30 years of experience in working directly with teachers and principals in building inclusive literacy practices for all students, especially students with disabilities and English language learners. Her experiences range from classroom teacher to union president and department chair, to professional development specialist and anti-racist educator. Since 1994, she has developed and taught a course for teachers and administrators titled "Anti-Racism and Effective Classroom Practices," and she has created several models of diversity training for students. Ms. Mata Aguilar brings to her work the bilingual and bicultural perspective of growing up Chicana in southern Texas's Rio Grande Valley. Currently, she directs three federally funded projects. *Partners: Building Co-Teaching Practices in Inclusive Middle Schools* has developed and will disseminate a model for building schoolwide co-teaching practices through a mutually supportive partnering of two middle schools. *Good High Schools: Describing and Validating Results for Students with Disabilities* has selected three urban high schools that demonstrate positive academic performance and outcomes for students with disabilities. *ICARE Schools: A Research Study of Meaningful Parent Involvement in the IEP Process* will identify middle schools that engage traditionally marginalized parents of students with disabilities in meaningful ways.